THE NEW
ROMANTIC GARDEN

THE NEW ROMANTIC GARDEN

Jo Thompson

RIZZOLI
NEW YORK

New York · Paris · London · Milan

Contents

6 Introduction
A Garden of One's Own

26 Historic Kent Estate
A Patient Intervention

36 Order in Disorder
Fairies at the Bottom of the Garden

46 Water as Muse
Surprise in the City

52 Riverside Haven
Exquisitely Small and Secret

60 Engineering as Art
A Pavilion of Curves

66 In Tune with the Land
Quiet Structure

76 A Writer's Retreat
Summer Solstice

84 Naturalistic Garden
Seeing the Vision

94 Gathering All
Pub Garden

102 Collaboration
Making a Garden with an Architect

108 Winter Solstice
A Barn for All Seasons

114 Rural Sussex
Blossom in Frost

122 Writer's Garden
Spring Equinox

130 Beltane
Rising Energy

136 Wild for Wildlife
A Garden of Neighbours

142 Rose-Lover's City Garden
When a Garden Looks Inwards

150 Chatsworth House
Revelling in a River

158 Georgian Townhouse
Embracing History

166 Sussex Beach Garden
Always on Display

172 A Spot for Sport
Two Dreams in One Design

180 Conjuring Reality
Making a Show Garden

186 Three Inspirations
Venetian Colour

192 Irises Galore
A City Jewel

200 Look Beyond
A Penthouse Garden

206 Every Shade of Green
Placemaking for Leisure

214 Outdoor Art Gallery
Secret Garden in Kent

220 Cabinet of Curiosities
A Coastal Sussex Garden

224 Water Lane
*Restoring a Victorian
Walled Garden*

234 A Historic Village Garden
Repairing the Land

240 RHS Rosemoor
A Garden within a Garden

246 Acknowledgments

247 Photography Credits

A Garden of One's Own

Gardens stay in the memory. Whether a small square patch of soft green English lawn or the dry springy grass of a garden in Tuscany, coarse underfoot and as tough as anything, green spaces associated with a moment in time hold their texture forever. The mind may record daisies everywhere, roses everywhere.

Blurrily romantic impressions of the bluster and gusts of a Cornish headland, rhododendron dens sliding down a Dorset chine, or the surprise of a back door opening onto a Norman motte. Childhood awe at Villa d'Este's five hundred fountains, segueing seamlessly into teenage disinterest in the roses and hydrangeas shaping the borders created by my parents.

The first garden I created was my own, on a roof in West London. I knew that there was a surface I could stand on up there, and I had an idea that this space would change the quality of life lived in cramped quarters below. But how to go about transferring into three dimensions the space's potential energy, how to achieve a vague idea of a romantic landscape a world away from pavement stone and tarmac? It had me foxed.

I knew I wanted pretty, a surprise, a small but welcoming place where friends could come and relax and get their fresh-air fix and nature's vitamin shot. I went over to the nearby garden nursery and asked if they could help me. The man I was talking to started drawing on a pad and when I asked him what he was doing he said, "I am designing your garden." This was the first light bulb moment for me.

Some thirty years later, this fascination with enhancing a space's potential until it's able to romance every single visitor wraps itself up and around my mind with every new garden. It isn't a complete image that forms in my head when I visit a new project, no strict planting plans pop up to delineate the space neatly. But there's something. It's an atmosphere, a sense of the window box, courtyard, lawn, doorstep, landscape, balcony, terrace, meadow, or whatever outside space it may be, being enjoyed, used, loved, and most importantly to me, forming the backdrop for life's moments and for people's own garden memories. All these ideas and more rush round my head as I decide first and foremost how the garden tells me it wants to *feel*.

Fast-forward past designs and hauling hardwood panels up the façade of a building on the windiest of days; these people created for me a beautiful haven amongst the chimney pots of Maida Vale. This was my first experience of seeing someone transform a space specifically to a person's taste. I was smitten and, pregnant with my first child, I spent the spring dragging bags of compost and trays of bedding plants up five flights of stairs to tend to my precious oasis, which was both my retreat and my place to share. I found that this work was surprisingly fun, and I still maintain today that a space in the open air of one's own should never carry with it the sense that there are chores attached. To-do lists, yes: pruning and weeding and clearing, but these words become *tending* and *composting* and *liberating*. There's a direct result and reward for cold winter days spent doubled over and a frankly brilliant sense of smug self-satisfaction every spring.

Page 6: A tangle of roses in a corner of the author's garden.
Page 7, left: *Rosa* 'Ghislaine de Féligonde'. Page 7, right: *Rosa* 'Adélaïde d'Orléans'.
Opposite: *R.* 'Adélaïde d'Orléans' tumbles over a garden gate.

Attraction

My garden today is in a village—the best of all worlds. The lifestyle here enticed me with its promises: just near enough to neighbours, only a short walk to the greengrocers and fields and lakes for dog walks long and short. The sound of eighteenth-century church bells cast by Thomas Janaway and an even older graveyard grazed by sheep. Continuing the romance by representing a sense of that same attractive place within my own garden was what came next. It's easy enough to carry out research in the place where I live: every day is a site study. Hedgerow plants are absorbed into the memory along with a general sense of what feels *right*—it's hard to go *wrong* in understanding where you are.

Respecting the location and applying that respect are something else, though. Every time a pastel Provençal courtyard or the Majorelle blue, whose intensity can only be gauged against the Moroccan sky, tempts you as inspiration in a more temperate climate, take yourself firmly in hand and have a quick walk around the block. See what you feel like when you get home again. Will that colour really work against grey British or New England skies? Will an exotic marble survive frosts that go on and on and on? Glass half-full always, I never outright dismiss a client's requests; instead I examine and extrapolate, prod and investigate and ponder until we get to the *feeling* at the centre of the wish. There's a lot to be said for simply sharing a cup of tea over these initial discussions. I'm still having cups of tea decades later with some garden owners; the conversation continues as the garden grows and changes, and from this process emerges friendship, such a hard thing to pin down. Excited chats and sometimes head-scratching

puzzling over an ailing plant that really should have worked according to my experience, plant trials studied, books read, and experts consulted. Because let's face it, sometimes plants simply don't like where we stick them. A garden is never going to stay static, and the conversation of trust that comes out of honesty is a long one as we observe watching the changes, the zooming forwards and the hesitations as the garden is hit by a random extreme weather variation, and the following recovery.

And that cup of tea is where it all starts. We get to know each other, and I get to understand what is required of the garden, but more vitally than that, I get to know the garden's owner. I can test out ideas and gauge the responses, and whilst I can gently push a solution, illustrating it in picture and word, I'm never going to force it if it doesn't sit well. The bottom line is that I do not want anyone to be thinking "that bloody garden designer" five years later when they look at an area they just knew they'd never like or use but which I'd convinced them to put in. Gardens borne out of a basis of an emerging friendship are satisfying places.

And it isn't too hard to get to a place that suits both parties. Walls of ultramarine and floors of pale tumbled stone are, it turns out, usually associated with a happy holiday, warm weather, family, delicious food, new friends, snapshots, laughter, and relaxed days that melt into relaxed evenings. We can take all these sensations and translate them from a foreign tongue into the foundation of a new domestic garden while making it the best, most authentic version of itself. I look at the garden, fix it firmly in my eye, and assure it that *it's very much not about me, it's about you.*

Opposite: One of my favourite rambling roses, *Rosa* 'Adélaïde d'Orléans', with its tumbling clusters of blooms, is perfect for pergolas and arches.

Overleaf: The romance of the rose remains strong. From left to right,
R. Port Sunlight (= 'Auslofty'), *R.* 'Ispahan', and
R. Munstead Wood (= 'Ausbernard').

Integrity

Where my cottage is, in a village already surrounded by houses of brick and tiles, there was once a yard for a stonemason. It's a veritable mini quarry, so as I occasionally unearth leftover lumps of stone, I opt to make them part of the garden. A reimagined rockery is the usual terminus for chunks of ragstone; an outsize piece of York stone that is suspiciously six feet long and two and a half feet wide now leads the way horizontally along the garden path. The original part of the once two-up/two-down dwelling has stone hearths completely out of scale with the diminutive size of the rooms. The theme continues on the interior. As with a lover, we can sense innately whether a garden feels genuine, stable, true.

When I first arrived here there was no garden as such, just a grassy drive with bare fences and peculiar trellis panels erected at points where it seemed that privacy had been needed. Strange diagonals were formed by the walls that held up the garden's higher level, diagonals then contradicted by a curving path slicing along the central axis, optimistic lavender edging on heavy Wealden clay. Nothing related to anything else.

Yet I recognised that the garden was in a pretty place, so I didn't want to hide that place, I wanted to celebrate it. The eastern view is the best view I have, and it dictates this garden. There's a sense of who and what has gone before as the church, whose layout dates from the twelfth century, creates one of the focal points of the garden. How did they live? What did they grow? What has happened here? All these questions are lined up with how I want my garden to be: full of softness, catching the sunrise, a place to grow and record plants that are allowed to grow and tangle into each other. I might not know much of this actual place's history, but I am surrounded by the history of the place, and from this, all else comes.

I looked kindly, therefore, on an old, badly pruned copper beech just to the east of the ugliest of fences. I'd had a pretty good idea that the sun would rise beyond its leaves and catch both them and the church spire, assets. But how to distract attention from the plainest of boarded boundaries? If I couldn't hide this ugly fencing, I could instead create something else in the foreground that would be much more interesting to the gaze. This was a cue to take a look around, to see what was happening beyond my boundaries.

Simple souls, often where we are looking is where we are thinking. If we don't look directly at ugliness, we won't think about it. A screen isn't always the best way to hide something if all it does is make us wonder what it's hiding, so it's often better to make everything else look fabulous to halt the gaze, holding it and bending it away.

Opposite: *Rosa* Munstead Wood (= 'Ausbernard') (left) and
R. 'Bobbie James' (right), are just two of the many roses in my own cottage
garden in the heart of Sussex.

Depth

Layers add depth, complexity, enduring interest to a garden; they also act as frames, catching our eye in the best ways. In a small country garden, the vernacular sets my way. Contemporary glass and steel do not belong here; chestnut, oak, and clay are the skeleton for layers of green. Good bone structure that recedes under a riot of green and attention-grabbing blooms in foliage months is what I wanted.

The layers that weren't too nice—those diagonals and curves switching and winding and fighting against each other—were the first things to go. This also meant abandoning the established but awkward line of desire (usually useful and sensible); I redirected the path to the front door so it took a longer way round, right along that nasty fence. This seems counterintuitive, making the everyday approach longer and darker, so I had to make this route one that people would want to take.

If a route to somewhere is attractive and easy to navigate, and if the destination is appealing, you'll gladly use it. Pretty obvious, really. So how to do that? My answer—here and often since—was to use roses. Roses everywhere: vertical, horizontal, wherever they would go. I'd identified three rather sad *Rosa* 'Bobbie James' ramblers previously shoved in along the fence line, and wanting to work with these poor little specimens, I put up a chestnut pergola to run along this new path to the house and then clothed it with climbing plants. This frame turns as the path turns, taking you along and through a tunnel of leaves, so that you're never quite sure when you're going to arrive as evergreen shrubs fill the spaces between the timber uprights. Yes, it takes a little longer, but when you emerge in June with a sprinkling of petal confetti, you know it's worth it.

This wooden structure is the only structure in my garden. There's nothing else—no expensive garden building, no smart terrace. Just a walkway of sometimes flowers and oftentimes leaves, all sitting just below the line of borrowed rooftops that form the background layers.

Intoxication

As a garden designer's own garden is destined to be a place of experimentation and observation, I determined to include my own library of plants that I could refer to as I help other gardens grow. It's a specialist library: a collection of plants selected for the simple reason that I love them, grown because I've become intoxicated with their colour or form or scent. They make me happy, and I want others to experience the same, satisfying feeling when what you've planted grows and forms part of the jigsaw of the atmosphere. Every plant in your garden should have a detail that makes you fall in love with it too. Anything that is too high maintenance, however, is given to friends with full disclosure. I need to be able to assure my clients that if I can grow whatever I'm proposing, then so can they.

If a cobbler's children are said to have no shoes, I had to embrace the fact this meant that my profession would dictate my own too-numerous plant children probably not ever having proper permanent beds to sleep in. Once I realised my garden needed to change more than most, however, I got to where I wanted: a romantic place full of changing plants spotted and dotted and located in the unlikeliest of places.

In this cottage garden, memory and nostalgia play a large part in what goes in and what comes out in other gardens: storybook roses and columbines feel as if they belong. Apart from the thorns of the roses, all is soft and tumbling, as plants are left to explore where they want to go. Irises have made their way happily under the shade of shrub roses who have climbed into the shade of trees—lots of rule-breaking going on. Plants have their places but they also surprise us, and tolerance is the approach in these beds.

Even before it had a name, no-dig has always been my approach—I worked out a long time ago that if I turned the soil, the weeds followed. (The brutal truth is that there's little time for many hours of maintenance, and if I can see a corner to be cut, I'll cut it.) So a thick mulch of compost is added each year, over the tulip bubs that I've forgotten to plant. As the ground is now too hard, the bulbs are placed on the surface, and covered with the compost. (I have to admit it can make for a rather rocky tulip; the risk is totally yours.) No chemicals either, for the simple reason that I don't want to breathe them in or touch them, and I don't want to inflict ingestion on anything else living either. Slugs then think they can get away with it, but there are several lines of defence in this garden: wool pellets, copper tape and copper mesh fences around raised beds and pots, and, I confess, it's all washed down with beer and an occasional sprinkle of salt.

Ornamental grasses have their place if they deserve it. Anything with too surprising a form (e.g., miscanthus) are excluded, spots going instead to anything that creates a veil: *Molinia caerulea* subsp. 'Transparent' is as its name suggests, *Sporobolus heterolepsis* provides a lower-level gauze, while fuzzy feather tufts of *Calamagrostis brachytricha* bring autumn hope. Three huge *Stipa gigantea* wave about amongst a collection of English roses. Each year I threaten to remove these grasses, as their broken stems require frequents trips with the secateurs, but each year they win a stay of execution as their giant oats look for all the world as if they were born to be arranged alongside the roses' full-fat contrasts.

Meadows of bulbs and buckets of tulips and
hyacinths brighten up the grey days of spring.

In summer, butterflies and bees congregate in the mass planting of buddleja
in this wild corner, whilst at a lower level, hedgehogs and toads can take refuge
in the deliberately untidy planting.

Friendship

One of the thrills of growing plants, getting to know them and understanding them, talking about them (and yes, sometimes *to* them), is finding like-minded people. People who approve of you growing your roses across the window so they look like wallpaper from the inside out. People who procrastinate and still haven't planted their tulips and it's *January*. People who believe pansies have faces and foxgloves are fairy skirts.

This garden is also full of a different type of flower friends: the plants themselves. All of them mean something to me and are extremely dear—apart from the bindweed, whose naughty little shoots, falsely unassuming-looking until they decide to make a break for it, I do take exception to. The names of roses conjure up romantic histories; I praise them for their beauty and commend them for their bravery when they throw out bonus blooms in October. I console them and remind them of their resilience when summer rain ruins the buds they've spent so long making. I remind them that the aphids will soon go, and sure enough they vanish overnight as the fledgling bluetits earn their wings, their feathery rounds bright boroughs among the mother-of-pearl globes of *Rosa* The Lark Ascending (= 'Ausursula') that sits in view of my kitchen sink.

The roses surrounding the breakfast terrace are good companions, to me and to each other. The end of May signals their arrival, Falstaff (= 'Ausverse') in deepest red, Munstead Wood (= 'Ausbernard') the same but different, deliberately placed against peach Port Sunlight (= 'Auslofty') and pink 'Ispahan'. They merge with the giant oat grasses that make three breaks in this high hedge of roses: a hedge to stop people falling off the higher level onto the stone slabs below, a raised planter providing me with nose-height scent, and colour.

Just beyond them, *Rosa* 'Blush Noisette' climbs up to lintel height: she won't go much higher but is just right here where the tile-hung wall of the next floor up precludes any climbers. Pushing out flowers till Christmas, she deserves a medal for her tenacity. At her feet, *Geranium* 'Catherine Deneuve' is all willowy elegance as she scrambles through the wallflowers alongside her more stately but also more sociable friend, *Geranium* 'Rozanne', the first of the cranesbills to arrive at the party and often the last to leave.

Rosa 'Meg' climbs by the door. Inspired by the colour magic of this rose against the range at Sissinghurst, I relaxed my suspicion of modern climbers and brought her in. She climbs too high for this little cottage, so many of her stems need lopping off, but she's forgiving of this and in compensation I allow the pink-orange flowers to become pear-shaped hips, their colour echoing early tulip tones below.

Every tulip is my favourite—there is no shame here in swapping loyalties fluid and fickle as earlies, mids, and lates dawdle or dash (depending on the variety) through and around the garden, changing each year as I play with new colour palettes and trial unknown beauties. Relatively inexpensive, the year's bulbs are eventually moved along to the vegetable patch, allowing those who are so inclined to bloom the following year, colouring the beds before I bring the stems into the house. Sustainability, regeneration, waste not want not, lies at the heart of all.

One of the joys of planting tulips is the range of atmospheres and effects
you can create by using different colour schemes.

Mood Lighting

Shades, tones, hues—what I see versus what you see in each flower very much depends on where you view it from. It's only when you've grown a plant, known a plant, that you know how it behaves in terms of colour reproduction. Different lights do have impact. In this garden, asters colourshift according to their spot: under a silver birch they are individual sparkles, whilst in brighter positions their flowers merge to form a mass.

The grasses are set where they will catch the light. Quick smiles of summer lightning flit and play on the flowers so that their tone shifts along creating their very own colour chart, catching and holding on to the light, blurring all in the most relaxed of ways. Their height doesn't mean relegation to the back row; in a cottage garden setting, if this is what this garden is, the atmosphere can be softened and relaxed by bringing the grasses forward, thinking about the sun and how it's going to move across the space. Here, the *Stipa gigantea* were positioned so that they would catch the early rays from the east as the sun appears from behind the now-invisible fence.

Courtship

Part of romance is allowing nature to dictate how relationships—between people, between plants, between plants and people—develop. Manicured neatness has its place; that place is not this garden. Not in a village that encourages daily ambles to admire the rambling ways it has itself grown and changed over centuries. Aside from the fact that the beds are places for experiments in companionship and performance as species court each other, I have to accept the gardener that I am: somewhat fairweather and with never enough time. Combine this with my urge to have as many plants as I possibly can within the space, with not enough regard to planting rules, and the relaxed "style" emerges.

It's been a way of approaching planting since I first started to grow plants, and this suits me. I'm not a great follower of "fashionable" plants either; my tiny rebellion is to champion the unfashionable. I've been growing dahlias for years and I've been on a mission to persuade many that hydrangeas are exactly what's needed. And for variegation—what exactly is wrong with *Euonymus fortunei* 'Emerald Gaiety'? It brightens up an otherwise unplantable spot in my garden. I want to see the plants enjoying themselves, scrabbling and climbing where they shouldn't but they do. In one large bed, *Rosa* 'Mary Rose', 'Eglantyne', and 'Gentle Hermione' form a pink structure in front of three tree peonies that have yet to flower. I wait patiently and admire their leaves instead. I wonder how much longer to give them, but I'm soon distracted by the exquisite bowls of 'Gentle Hermione' flowers. Following on from the roses' first flush, with *Iris* 'Jane Phillips' and *Papaver* 'Patty's Plum' over, eupatorium and *Ammi majus* create new height, coming up from whichever geranium has won the battle for space at the time.

I like to let the plants define the space how they choose. Less control means a different expression and a different atmosphere each year as one plant thrives better than another according to the weather. A warm, wet summer produces the hugest of hydrangea panicles whilst the roses think about coming back out; blasting heat makes the Joe Pye weed seriously consider its existence and the cosmos take over instead.

The roses actually smother the thankfully-chunky walkway. *Rosa* 'Adélaïde d'Orléans' and

21

R. 'Félicité-Perpétue' are joined by others that I didn't know so well. 'The Albrighton Rambler' (= 'Ausmobile') is a winner, climbing and blooming pink till the end of the season. A darkish corner surprises me each year as 'Snow Goose' (= 'Auspom') thrives in the shade of the copper beech. I suggest to it that its stems go around the timber upright, a job not to be done in haste, but the stems are malleable and winding them around and around means that I get tiny buds of pink and cream at eye level, with flowers into November. Just behind it is a clematis, name forgotten and label lost, which is a mass of green on the ugly fence, but only leaves. No flowers appeared in seven years, probably due to the grim conditions, but it charms me as it scrambles and escapes up into the tree's branches before dangling down again over the rockery's evergreen ferns. And a few years after that, the same clematis rewards my patience by revealing a mass of creamy-white bell-shaped flowers, announcing itself as C. 'Wisley Cream'.

The garden lets it all hang out a bit. The lawn is clover, meaning less mowing and more bees. Dandelions are tolerated, as is herb-Robert. *Erigeron karvinskianus* is allowed to self-seed, as is the *Briza media* that first entered as one quaking head in a pot and has now colonized wherever it can. It gets pulled up in winter as its stems become murky, but I know the seeds will reappear. *Verbena bonariensis* is another prolific self-sower here, yet however much I encourage fennel to throw itself around, it refuses. A work in progress.

Intrigue

As I plan an outside space, the journey around the garden has to reveal itself—gradually and with intrigue as a motivating factor for the visitor. In romance, the unknown keeps us interested. *Where am I going? Why? What is it going to be like when I get there? Will I want to stay there, or move on? How easy will that be? Will it all have been worth it in the end?* All tied up with the atmosphere of a romantic place, the sense of what it was and what it could be, this route-planning is something to get right, right at the start.

We are suggestible—we see something, then we see it somewhere else, and we connect the two. Dot-to-dot for grown-ups, we're relieved to see these mindmarks as they tell us what to do. A couple of pots mark the front door, another pot placed to one side might lead us to another door.

In this mass of plants, the roses landsliding into view form these visual cues, leading you along the path, around the corner and down some steps to the entrance to the house. In the place that it is, I felt this garden wasn't the right home for primly trimmed topiary. The formality of clipped beech or yew would have probably worked—but it's simply that the place is too small. I could easily go overboard, but grand scale would I feel lead to a sense of ostentation in this little village garden. I keep looking beyond, out, and over, and ask myself what feels right. It's as simple an approach as that.

Commitment

Whether it is a Humphry Repton landscape or a modern urban scene in a tiny space, the obvious and great thing about gardens is that they are living things. Stones and bricks are generally set as they are, but even the most historic gardens need to change as things grow and die, and we have to accept that our relationship with a garden will also evolve as we commit to caring for it over many years. By this very nature of affairs, creating or renovating a garden is about capturing an "essence," not being bound by history and what has gone before, but respecting it, evolving and adding something of the times we live in now to it.

It often boils down to the fact that less in terms of designed elements is nearly always more. It may seem a cliché, but Alexander Pope's "consult the genius of the place in all," taken from the Romans, are surely some of the wisest words in landscape design. Would my little worker's cottage ever have had the occasion to host the formal yews of the rectory just beyond? Almost certainly not—this would have been a place for growing vegetables with perhaps a flower or two for prettiness. But this leads to another issue: I am not creating a pastiche, wherever I am working. The garden doesn't need to be a replica of a Georgian cottage garden. It doesn't need to look as if it's been there forever. But it needs to look as if it *should* be there, *today*.

So I take another look. Here I look at the rooftops, at the church and the trees. I truly do immerse myself in the place, gather in the atmosphere and think about who and what has gone before, who and what is to come, and how to romance everyone into lingering.

Overleaf: A simple combination of allium and camassia
provide cheerful colour in late spring.

The Gardens

A Patient Intervention

This pair of herbaceous borders was looking truly magnificent in scale, if not in content, when I saw them for the first time—ironic since I had just been invited to revitalize them for a new century. Scale lent a lot to that impression. They travel the length of an avenue, north to south, delineated by an arboretum to one side and an Edwardian rose garden to the other. Structure planned a hundred years ago still endured: camellia, styrax, magnolia, azara, and azaleas. Special, interesting, specimens suggested that someone had once truly loved this garden. It posed an interesting challenge of how to proceed, and I knew that no matter what my revisions, I would also play just a temporary role in this garden's ongoing legacy. It would continue to change after me. Of course; it's a living garden.

For a place with so much history, I start by looking for snippets and stories, clues to the original designer's intent. I try to absorb whatever secrets the remaining plants whisper to me. Magnolias still tower along the borders' borders, in particular a *Magnolia campbellii* 'Betty Jessel', with slate-black buds and flowers of striking crimson and ruby. Overgrown shrubs and colour given mainly from green and from glimpses of flower petals peeking through the gaps in surrounding foliage otherwise created a fuzz of pink that bled out to deep wine. I realised that, with these borders, there was nowhere to hide—the person who first laid them out rather cleverly arranged paths along the back of them too, so that they could be admired from every angle.

It was time to gently nudge these deep borders into the twenty-first century, while respecting who and what had come before. A simple combination of perennials creates a wash of colour, whilst a clipped berberis provides structure in the background.

Top: *Magnolia campbellii* 'Betty Jessel'. Above: *Rosa* Mary Rose (= 'Ausmary'). Opposite: *Cirsium rivulare* 'Atropurpureum' gives height and informal structure to the border.

Overleaf: Traditional perennials feel as much at home in a small cottage garden as they do here. Spires of digitalis, campanula, and delphinium balance the roundness of the roses' flowers.

During research trips to archives, a bit of delving around boxes, and lots of Googling, I learned some very fascinating facts about the Jessel family's original garden plans. I found a report on that majestic magnolia stating that it originated as a seedling obtained by Sir George Jessel from the Lloyd Botanic Gardens, Darjeeling, in 1937. Yet according to Sir George's son, Sir Charles Jessel, his father asked Marchants Nursery of Wimborne to obtain the plant from Darjeeling, which was then planted in the 1950s and named after his wife in 1967. Whatever its origin, with that much family interest it was clear the cultivar needed to maintain pride of place in a contemporary scheme. You might be lucky, as I was, and find an Ordnance Survey map made by a cartographer who happened to be a fan of gardens. I spend a lot of time looking at old maps and I'm convinced that, to an extent, the detail of a historic map skews in line with the hobbies of the map-maker on duty on a particular day. One map will show only the simplest outline of a garden whilst another looks as if it was prepared for posterity, with all trees and buildings carefully labelled. Digging up these little history-hinges should be the first sort of digging any designer does.

You're lucky if you find diary entries of an event in a garden from a hundred years ago—novels are where we usually find romantic occurrences set in a garden—but sometimes archives have been preserved and you can spend happy days poring through correspondence and sketchbooks. More often than not, of course, a garden's history is left to the imagination. Hours spent getting to know a place *do* create a story in the mind, however, and it's to that main plot we can add the twists and details. Garden designers' characters are trees and plants, but they have every bit as much individual personality as the heroes and villains of literature.

I like to think about how people in generations before might have moved along this same border. Did someone stand in my exact spot and admire the development of a tree they had planted? Did someone have an assignation here, even, when it all was blooming with heady scents and impossibly romantic?

I envision babies then, adults now, toddling alike down the lawned path. Density, formality, romance, light and shade, movement, and eye-catching blooms all combine into a unique setting very capable of influencing our human actions. Distilling how all these interact defines what a place actually is, what it should be. Whilst I know this sounds vague and intangible, it does happen as you allow yourself time to absorb a garden's essence.

Here, I was lucky enough to find another map dating to the 1870s, when someone else had made an excellent record of the border. The key thing for me was finding out that these borders had been there for a long time, long enough to cement them as integral to the property. The specimen plants that I found suggested a true garden lover. In a 1957 *Country Life* article, Christopher Lloyd attributed many specimen plant introduction and the creation of vistas to William Goldring, who he described as "a celebrated designer of the Edwardian period." Many of the existing trees had been there as long ago as 1904, according to photos I discovered. In front of the trees and shrubs, I could also make out low repeated herbaceous planting, all on the flat in front of a middle-storey shrubbery very much of its time. This garden had been created by generations of garden lovers—that much is historical fact.

Left: *Allium* 'Mt. Everest' and *Rosa* Mary Rose (= 'Ausmary') and *R.* Gertrude Jekyll (= 'Ausbord') pick up the light in this partially shaded spot.

Above, left: Hoops of rusted steel provide plant support in summer and sculptural structure in winter.

Above, right: Delphiniums planted towards the front of the border create a high veil through which the rest of the planting can be glimpsed.

But it was time to gently nudge these borders into the twenty-first century, while respecting who and what had gone before. I needed to take into consideration all the whispers and hints of their presence, from the garden itself to the ghosts of people who had loved it over decades—they weren't going to let me ignore them. And so, with the aim of doing something without looking like I'd done anything, I started to think about structure.

The outside edges of the border were all vertical fabulousness, so with a bit of tweaking and liberating, they had every right to stay. I began with the shrubs. You've got to love a flowering shrub. Or an evergreen shrub. Or all shrubs, every single one. I have felt very, very sorry for shrubs over the last quarter of a century. Sharp-elbowed out of favour by presumptuous ornamental grasses, they've been quietly biding their time in a Colefax and Fowler floral fabric kind of a way. Slowly and steadfastly though, both shrubs and chintz have come back around into fashion, appreciated again as fundamental backdrops in any solid design scheme. Roses followed by hydrangeas are a mainstay in the gardens I work in, and we need them here as well. I mean, can you imagine banks of on-trend panicum and calamagrostis sitting against this fabulous range of shrubs? Lovely in the right place for sure, but wrong for certain here. There were a group of massively overgrown, wild, unruly shrubs near the steps at the entrance to this area. Out-of-control, leggy, incomprehensible flailing mounds of berberis, euonymus, and pittosporum looked messy and annoying. The easy route would be to replace them all with smart domes of something.

I thought about it. And then the penny dropped: Why not wrestle and massage these shaggy beings into smart domes? Well, I could have a go. I always

Opposite: The vertical lines created by these plants' stems are echoed in the steel poles scattered through the border.

Right: Existing trees and shrubs provided the framework for the restoration of these historic borders

want to make do with what I've got wherever I can after taking stock of the stock, slash and burn being the last viable option.

And from that came almost instant structure. Structure that had always lain there below since that first intentional planting; it simply needed a bit of assistance in being liberated from the results of a lack of maintenance. However informal we want our garden to be, a garden is by its very nature something that will get out of hand if there is no structure, no gentle rules imposed. A careful editing process of pruning and trimming and stepping back and then going in again resulted in huge globes of green, white, purple. These now lead the eye here, then here, and then over here, relaxing focal points and quiet, necessary foils to the blousy looseness elsewhere. I did consider repeating the deep purple berberis further down these beds but I hesitated. Dark leaves can be a tricky old thing in the garden; in the wrong place they zoom your eye up to them quickly, so you end up missing what you should be looking at in between, as well as from a distance

reading as large black holes. Instead here I opted for softer shapes of purple, sometimes setting them back so that you don't see all this dark from everywhere.

The perennials are traditional. Nothing too exotic, many of the plants chosen would be as at home in a small cottage garden as they are here in this estate setting. Foxgloves, bellflowers, and delphiniums form spires that balance the fullness, the roundness of the roses' flowers, whilst dots of colour from the smaller flowers of hardy geraniums and astrantia create a wash of colour and texture between the architectural forms of cirsium and echinops. Drifts of each cultivar wind their way through, a touch of modernity introduced by bringing the taller plants nearer the front of the border instead of obeying the oft-repeated rule that tall plants should stay at the back of the border. The stems and the spires create the haze, a kind of a mist which stops the eye for a moment and lets it linger on what is there. A tumbling, full, and fresh border feels as modern as it does historical.

Fairies at the Bottom of the Garden

"Where does your planting style come from?" This is a question that's often put to me—how and why I put together collections of plants as I do. I want to put together plants that grow together, or that appear as if they *should* grow together. Plants that you'd expect to see side by side in their native environment, but with a twist: these aren't all natives. Some of them are, but others simply have distant native plant relatives. I seek out flower shapes recalling daisies and harebells—long, skinny stems that bring to mind shaggy hedgerows.

From the start, I had the very strong sense that a combination of these shapes and structures would aid obvious interlopers such as *Echinacea purpurea*, and larger blooms such as roses, in connecting with and holding on to their place. It is an atmosphere, a mood, a spirit that I want to harness when I'm putting a planting together. If there were a Venn diagram of these, all would overlap, overlay, intertwine so it felt just right at the centre. One doesn't come before the other. I'm hoping here that by singling out which comes where and how, separating out these strands, I'll go some way to clarify and pinpoint the key elements of this natural-looking, romantic style.

First, I want to make a garden that a bee will happily visit. That a caterpillar will feed on. That a butterfly will rest on. That aphids will come to so that the bluetits can eat them. You may be horrified by the mention of aphids, but if I don't have them, I won't have as many bluetits in my garden. Try it for yourself: Take the leap and leave those greenfly that

escape any spraying you might employ. I promise you that some beneficial creature will come along and find them: sparrows, ladybirds, hoverfly larvae. Natural predators miraculously discover that there's a food source for themselves and/or for their young, and so come and feast. And among these creatures, there's something else that's very present for me.

I know I run the risk of losing you here: What's not to say that there are fairies at the bottom of the garden?

I'm not talking about Victorian fairies here, all winged prettiness and darting sylphs. I'm talking about the sense of intangible presence, a sense that taps on my shoulders, nibbles at my subconsciousness when I'm standing within a planting that has grown up for the garden, grown for those who live here, and to a very small extent, grown for me. Nothing ever grows how I expect it to grow. I have an idea of what it's roughly going to look like, but I always know that nature will take what I bring and have her minions run away with it, making it her own, shifting and moving, encouraging and restraining as she sees fit. And as the garden grows, so its character develops and changes and decides what will suit it best. As gardeners we create the framework, we give the possibility, and then we hand it over.

This is the point where I say that the fairies come and take my trowel, but they more frequently take my secateurs. If you've ever had this happen to you, you'll know the feeling and have perhaps thought *Borrowers*. I promise you, in my garden they exist. I'll stare and stare at a spot where I put a brightly

Opposite: A path laid through abundant wildflowers creates a pleasant journey through the garden.

Overleaf: The wildflower areas of this garden also contain a few ornamental varieties; here the dark

stems of *Angelica sylvestris* 'Vicar's Mead' create an elegant silhouette.

coloured and thus distinctive pair of secateurs, and they're absolutely *not* there, absolutely, definitely and definitively not. I look away and look back again and they're back. How else do you explain that? Someone having a bit of fun with me, idle entertainment or testing my belief and respect, who knows? Maybe they then go and tell the bees to come, or the robin, perhaps, who clearly knows what I'm about to get up to as I walk outside. Put it down to madness, to an overactive imagination, but it's certainly a much more interesting explanation than plain-old forgetfulness.

Bear with me as I take us off into the realms of imagination and storytelling. Being a landscape designer involves inhabiting a fantasy world. I must always imagine a whole scenario parallel to the simultaneous reality—a more magical one in one way or another. As a firm supporter of anything that adds more colour to the world, you can imagine my delight when I stumbled upon the concept of fairy forts—ancient mounds associated with the fairy folk. You must never dare to build on one of these places, and even now their custodians protect them. (It may be that you're tapped for a couple of euros to pay out at the door, but it's all going to a good cause in my mind.) You only have to visit one of these ráths in Ireland for it to feel completely acceptable that these places should exist.

Above and right: The colours of this planting palette are kept deliberately muted so nothing distracts attention away from the gentle and natural atmosphere. Pale tones catch and hold onto the sunlight.

I get the same sense of ancient inhabitants as I visit this garden. Perhaps, who knows, we entered an unspoken pact, the clients and me, when we first started talking about it and making it, with many long discussions not about what we would touch but about that which we would leave be. Perhaps it was made for *them*, the little people that exist (albeit in my imagination) alongside the living things. I like to make for them a place of mystery, a place to hide themselves. I'm not talking about little winged fairies, precisely. I'm thinking about the spirit of the garden and the *spirits* of the garden, and how we should look after them, make them our friends. All the Good Folk who work for beauty.

If you're still with me, thank you for persisting. The further I explore this, the more I realise that when I look at this garden I can't help but see touch of real magic in it. I'll try to describe what I mean. It was made for a lover of the land, a lover of nature. As we talked and talked about the hopes for this landscape, we were weaving a kind of spell of Practicals and Fantasticals, with a great big dash of optimism and love added to the pot. Nothing that required too much fussy attention was to be included. We wanted to source plants locally, use local materials, and make do and mend wherever we could. People may not completely understand the word sustainability anymore, knowing only that it peppers sentences alongside biodiversity and climate change, but we've long been driven to be sustainable—we just need to recall and remember how, not be too seduced by the new unless it really has integrity, and work with what we can get from the land and what it can give back to us.

I'll work with the vernacular, for example, even if I have to go beyond a radius of fifteen miles to find the bricks or stone. Materials for gardens should be natural if possible. Anything that isn't just doesn't work in creating a feeling of helping the land along, and appears instead as a massive intervention. Designers say we don't want a space to reveal that we've had a hand in its development—it's getting a bit hackneyed now, but this was an honest response

Fairy Presence

There are thousands of fairy forts scattered around Ireland today, because *you must absolutely not* touch the homes of the fairies, or they will wreak revenge. These are the old homesteads of the Irish, known as "ring forts." They consist of a circular enclosure surrounded by an earthen or stone bank and they were designed to protect cattle at nighttime from raiders and wolves. As time passed, people moved out into more open forms of habitation; the fairies then moved in, making these ring forts their new homes. They are now called "fairy forts." The fairies are the greatest protectors of Irish archaeology because farmers refuse to touch these structures.

The whitethorn tree is also known as the "fairy tree." The fairies dance around them to celebrate the arrival of summer; if you have one on your land you leave it well alone so as not to upset "them that do be in it." Whitethorns are often used as hedgerows in Ireland, but a tree on its own in the middle of a field or a lone tree up the side of a hill is believed to have magical powers. There are thousands of fairy trees scattered around Ireland today, similarly left untouched because farmers are wary of cutting them down and upsetting the little folk.

Opposite, above: Whenever possible, I use trees and plants instead of hard materials to create architecture. Here, a grouping of roof-trained London plane trees provide shade and create a destination. Opposite, below: Ox-eye daisies have been allowed to stray from the meadow on the other side of the path.

43

here. I didn't want it to look as if I had been there. I didn't want to mess up the homes of those who live there, those whom I sense but don't see. And guess what? I might even ask their permission before I do go in. Again, I'm not talking about chants or potions, don't worry. It's simply about sitting in the space and allowing time to ascertain what feels right. Can I justify the imposition of X, the use of Y? If the answer isn't yes, then I know I have to forego those elements.

Wild spirits run through this garden, for sure. This look of wildness, of a connection with the natural, is something that I've been creating ever since I understood the concept of putting a few plants together. But I promise you, they are not "thrown" together. There's an order here, a process but not a system, and as that process changes for every garden, I'm not even sure that we can even call it that. An approach, then.

As an arrival, there's a sense of something that has been brought in: for example, low lumpy pillows of *Taxus baccata* sit at a key spot where all the entrance and exit routes converge, giving a visitor a number of choices as to where to go. Some call this a "decision point." I think of it as a moment to take a breather. The route opens up, closes, and opens up again, the clipped, firm topiary, in a space that's big enough for it, giving you permission to pause as you take it all in.

You're in the countryside here—ancient woodland holds this landscape in. Again, there's not only that sense of who and what has gone before, but also, really strongly, a sense of who and what is *still there*. Who knows what creatures still inhabit that landscape—dare I find out? My feeling is always that unless there's disease or danger, I should leave it be.

I remember talking through with the client the merits of each selected plant in the planting design. I love this stage of the process. (I love all stages, but this part is particularly exciting and whether plant lover or no, it's the point at which many clients start

to really "see" their future garden.) Long chats over those copious cups of tea discussing the beauty of a plant: a good way to spend a day. We came to *Eupatorium maculatum* 'Riesenschirm', Joe Pye weed, and conversation stalled. *Isn't it a weed? Isn't it a little dull? It's rather indistinct…Won't it take over?* For me, the answers are a resounding *No*. I plant this eupatorium at the backs of borders and at their fronts. Invertebrates adore it and it has such a lovely pinky-purple presence at a time when so many other things have vanished and others are just waiting to pop.

When I first saw this landscape, it was filled with human-imposed stuff: ornamental trees, hard lines of hard landscaping, hard lines of soft. What's wrong with that, you may ask—it's their own garden? But the whole place had an overwhelming feeling of being overworked. The skies were glorious; the setting is awe-inspiring Sussex at its most beautiful. Why force the gaze in rather than out? So fences were taken down, a meadow was encouraged, a stream was suspected, located, and restored. After these gentlest of interventions, taking out rather than putting more in, the place itself breathes more easily.

Now, based on a study of what occurs naturally in the surrounding area, native plants together with non-natives amble round in soft curves and tangling meadows in tune with the landscape beyond. Regeneration is at the heart of every gentle intervention. It is now a place for imaginative minds, a haven. Perennial meadow borders and perennial meadow beds keep the birds and the bees happy. We all have a responsibility to support species under threat, and simple steps make a tremendous difference. Each year, the owners and I check which species have thrived: the echinacea, which doesn't like it elsewhere in the same garden, absolutely adores being in this mix of perennials, among friends.

Clipped mounds of *Taxus baccata* form an island of structure, a foil to the waving wildflowers beyond.

44

Surprise in the City

This beautiful townhouse, owned by a truly wonderful family with young children, came with a garden that had nothing much to recommend it apart from its size, which is pretty great for London. It's forty-seven metres long and eleven metres wide, but was just a long rectangle of grass bordered by enormous, overgrown hedges and huge trees. The far end of the garden was completely overgrown and unusable. The family firmly believes that the garden should be for everyone, should draw generations together, and this is just one of the many reasons why we get on so well. We were in complete agreement about the fact that the garden should be for the parents, who want to entertain their family and friends and to spend more time learning how to develop their own gardening skills, as well as for the children. They wanted to enable their children to have a beautiful, inspirational space to play in, which hopefully would "by stealth" instil an absolute love of being outside, as the parents had their own memories of imaginative play and nostalgia for secret gardens. The main hopes were therefore to introduce a play structure, a dining terrace, and beautiful biodiverse plantings.

Even with a garden clearly ready for a complete renovation, as this one was, it's critical to sit with the space awhile, let the sense of it settle on you so you slow down to observe its light and shade and wildlife before embarking on any design. It's completely natural to want to get going straight away, but I urge you to fight the urge. Going through this process is a must. Every house is different, every client is different, every location is different—even

The family's children skip along this path, encountering moments of surprise along the way.

when they're next door to each other, which can often happen, as once a neighbour sees a garden—well, you can imagine. I go and spend a long old time rummaging around the garden at this early stage, absorbing the atmosphere, studying the site and the surroundings for clues as to history as well as botany and geology. In every garden, whether large or small, there is usually something to "borrow" from the landscape beyond. Those large trees, though they technically belong to neighbours, still provide a background layers of green. The neighbouring houses slightly overlook the garden, no surprise, so I also needed to create a sense of privacy, yet at the same time not impose too heavy a screen.

In considering elements that would delight different ages as well as give a sense of romantic adventure in an urban location, I found myself creating a sculptural route, a basaltite stone path winding its way like a river flowing through the garden, taking you to different eddies of surprise along the way that encourage you to slow down, notice, relax. It's the simplest, most organic of curves. It spills over from an elegant dining terrace and then flows across and along the site, this meandering in itself creating an exaggerated impression of space and heightening curiosity and interest as you potter along. I could envision children skipping along this path, or riding their little scooters, encountering moments of surprise on the way.

Above: The initial sketch for this family garden, meant to inspire play, shows my first ideas for a rill and pool; as the design progressed, these were replaced with water jets.

Right: An artful bench, sculptural as well as functional, appears in view as you walk along this garden's curved paths.

First you encounter pebble seats by the artist Ben Barrell—smooth, polished concrete sculptures. Placed against a soft, foliage-filled background, they become seating and art combined. Once I realised that I wanted to make the most of this idea of surprise, I pondered how I could tie in surprise with water, and this is where my years in Italy served as a direct influence. Thinking about the fabulous historic piazzas and villas and their elaborate fountains, I realised that I could incorporate surprise, play, and adventure by incorporating water jets in a sort of splash pad formation, and this is the second "surprise" along the path. A sculptural cantilevered bench in bronze resin here seems to float just above the nearby planting and serves as a place for adults to watch the children splash, or just to pause and watch the water alone. It's exciting when art can be interactive like this, designed to be used and climbed on, to have function

as well as form in a landscape. Travelling along, the "river" path eventually leads to a bespoke play structure at the far end of the garden. As the children grow older, the hedges in front of the structure will be allowed to grow taller and screen this large element, but for now, keeping them low means the children are visible from the house. Practicality reigns.

All of these hard elements do need a buffer layer of foliage and flowers, and even though planting design usually comes at the end of the garden design process, I have to emphasise how integral it is to any design. Over the last thirty years I have been bringing a softer, more romantic, "wilder" style to all the landscapes I create. It simply feels more natural. I work to combine traditional elements with new planting approaches to achieve a balance and a space that will stand the test of time. The lines within these gardens are softened by a mix of plants carefully selected for

Left: The idea of combining form and function continues here; the pebble sculptures provide somewhere to perch, somewhere to play.

Opposite: This is a garden for the whole family. A play structure tucked into its far end makes the most of every inch of the space. It includes a climbing frame, a rope walkway, a swing, and a slide.

the atmosphere they will create when put together. And of course, these plants need to be right for the location, easy to maintain, and be able to survive eventually without watering. The planting beds here are wide enough to allow for a depth of interest, and to balance everything else, as that path could otherwise dominate what the eye follows. The choice of plants stems from the atmosphere I want to create.

Surrounded by roses, this haven is tucked away enough to seem a secret garden, a surprise as well as a destination for those in the know. Boundaries between city and country are here blurred and lost.

There are English roses in rich red and softer pink shades: *Rosa* Munstead Wood (= 'Ausbernard'), *R.* (= 'Ausverse'), *R.* Gentle Hermione (= 'Ausrumba') are joined by *R.* 'Tuscany Superb' and *R.* 'Ispahan' for its entrancing scent. The roses are succeeded by hydrangeas for later colour in the garden; for all-year structure there are mounds of *Taxus baccata* and *Pittosporum* 'Golf Ball'. Then to the herbaceous perennials: there's a veil of planting here—tall plants with almost naked stems but hazy or petite, loose flowers—that forms a gauze over everything, gives height, and adds mystery and softness. *Cenolophium denudatum*, anthriscus, thalictrum. And of course, bulbs: tulips and alliums, replenished every year.

Essentially my approach to garden design has always been a gentle intervention rather than anything that reveals the heavy stamp of design. Each garden, in whatever country, needs to look as if it should be there. Energy and thought should manifest in romance, a story, a subconscious integrity. It begins by having a true respect for any space, no matter how you find it, and an understanding of what nature has already provided. It's thanks to forward-thinking clients who welcome ideas and go with concepts that might sound tricky to achieve, that I get to create some exciting gardens, gardens for young, middle-aged, and old that hopefully provide interest for everyone. Because of these trusting garden custodians, I get to share dreams that become part of life.

Exquisitely Small and Secret

"Make us want to go out into our garden." Not an unusual brief from clients, but in this case, the fact that a road separated the house from their primary outdoor space meant that they simply didn't want to go to all the effort of gathering up belongings, locking up one house, crossing a road, and unlocking a garden gate for the simple pleasure of going out into green.

This sense of separation changes everything that we know about what gardens need to do. Generally, the garden should have a sense of arrival, it should welcome you, offering tantalising glimpses of treasures and gems that lie just beyond, in order to entice you further.

In this garden however, there was none of that—just a forbidding dark gate set within a dark green yew hedge set on the other side of a well-used street. You might embellish the entrance to a traditional garden with a symmetrical arrangement of pots, say, or an asymmetrical-but-still-balanced planting of evergreens. This would create a sense of arrival, the signal that this is the way, that the garden wants you to come and explore further.

Yet here, the opposite is true. Since the gate is on a public thoroughfare, with no pavement outside, there's no possibility of placing welcoming containers of inviting shrubs. Added to this is the fact that you absolutely want to conceal the existence of the garden, to deter nosy passersby. No hints of planterly delights to beckon, hints of a hidden, secret garden to discover. It needed to be only for those who knew it was there.

A simple bench placed under an existing holly creates a destination out of a shady corner in a small city garden.

This entailed a total rethink and readjustment of my approach to design, which in itself is another glorious segment of the process of designing gardens. The constant idea of the new: new ways of thinking, new approaches to new problems, old stories to be told in a new way. No garden is the same, no client is the same, no house is the same, so why should two designs be similar? Admittedly it would make far more sense business-wise to churn out the same garden, adjusted for each space, but in my heart I've always known that this wouldn't be doing right by any garden, and my intention is always to create the space that I believe the place deserves.

I stood by the low wall that separates this garden from the River Thames as it flows through the heart of busy London. To one side, there was water, light, trees on a riverbank beyond. There was life as herons and moorhens made their way by, one swooping,

bobbing, each in their own particular style. There was life as skinny rowing boats skimmed past, propelled by eight exhausted rowers, urged on by a cox barking instructions at them through a megaphone.

On the other side, that dark green hedge loomed, separating this space from what lay in that direction. I talk of looking at what lies beyond as integral to the success of a garden. In this case, though, I realised there were two "beyonds"—one full of life, one closed off. This would need to be a secret garden with a twist, celebrating both the openness and the closed, with a sense of mystery that would be seen in the owners' imagination and therefore lure them in. It would be glimpsed by those out on the river—they would know it was there as they pottered or raced by, but they wouldn't be able to enter. And many simply wouldn't know it was there at all.

Have you ever looked at your own garden, or a scrap of land that you've been asked to design, and tried to tell yourself that small is beautiful, that size doesn't matter? That it simply doesn't matter that you don't have room for stuff, that there's simply nothing to be done with it as there's absolutely nowhere to hide?

The last part of that sentence is true; in a small garden design, there is indeed nowhere to hide your mistakes. Every error glares out at you, reminding you of the folly of perhaps trying to squeeze everything in,

or maybe ignoring certain factors in the surroundings, hoping that you can ignore them, mentally if not physically. And it's not through any lacking on your part—the smallest gardens are by far and away the hardest. Every tiny element gets scrutinised; everything can be seen at once.

When I first arrived here, I was met by a falling-apart and terrifyingly slippery terrace, an equally-falling-apart trellis, some fairly joyless paving blocks and a couple of out-of-place spiky plants which offered nothing of beauty nor of

Left and above: This garden was arranged to feel welcoming and to take advantage of the fabulous view. The curved bench is surrounded by *Hydrangea arborescens* 'Annabelle', planted to create a kind of nest.

environmental benefit. No pollen, no nectar, nothing. The lines of the garden were confusing: there were the pointy, sharp lines of collapsing balustrade, the amorphous lines of a path and diagonal lines of the terrace. The whole garden appeared to have been laid out on a day when decision-making had been difficult.

When faced with a collection of minus-points as large as this, it's time to think instead about all the positives. Here it was: the view. Probably one of the best views of all the very best London views, this garden is tucked in along the banks of the river as it snakes its way from one side of the city to the other. The water doubles the shifting scene as the

sky changes the picture every day. And actually, on inspection, whoever had originally set out the garden had successfully identified the best areas for views, and had taken a stab at making these spots into hospitable spaces. The problem was that they had then promptly forgotten the meaning of hospitality, using uncomfortable angles and unwelcoming thresholds that in fact shouted "keep out." I needed to reinterpret this as "come hither" instead.

The route round any garden space is important, and sharp rectilinear lines here would have been silly—people would cut corners as they always do with right angles in small gardens. A winding route would be a better solution, with plenty of alluring stopping-off

Opposite: *Rosa* Emily Brontë (= 'Ausearnshaw') marks the entrance to an archway filled with more blooms.

Above: Even a small garden can include a range of seating options, some secluded, others more open, as here.

moments along its way. Keeping things simple, I created a route easy to understand and therefore easy to use, with little offshoots of magic, which in themselves would hopefully create little moments of joy. Identifying those brilliant-but-unused spots and making them better means that they'll be utilised. And using all that volume of the space in this seemingly small garden makes room for more plants.

These moments of magic quickly started to identify themselves as the seating areas, and sometimes even as the routes and thresholds themselves to these areas. It didn't need to be overcomplicated. Make the path into a tunnel which opens out onto the view, framing it but also creating a sense of wonder in the actual act of opening out onto the terrace. Make that raggedy old holly tree into a better shape, and carve out a spot beneath it. Make the most of all the possible views and viewpoints—after all, that's what this garden was about.

To accommodate the curves of the path, small brick-like pavers were used, but larger paving was needed for the raised dining area, as small paving units lead to slight level changes and thereby to wobbly furniture, annoying to all. Even if you think you might be able to tolerate this wobbliness, all you have to do is imagine sitting down at that table in a pub—you lean forward to have a chat and suddenly, almost silently but very definitely, there's that tiny-yet-surprisingly-assertive clunk, which absolutely will not go away, however much you try to tolerate it and ignore it. The folded beermat is the only option. And you don't want to use folded beermats in your garden. Not on a daily basis, at any rate. Here, slabs of York stone laid in a random pattern proved strong enough to deal with the space and yet unobtrusive in colour and tone.

For the boundaries, timber trellis, with swooping swags of curves carved out so as not to block the view, creates the opportunity for that most romantic of features: the archway of roses, which entices you to keep moving along the path. This tunnel is also a double layer of privacy, another set of verticals to sit alongside the new vertical of the trellis, soon to be clad itself in roses along with clematis and evergreen climbers. Another of its functions is the way it also creates the threshold, that idea of something closing in and then opening up onto another scene.

The walkway, this threshold, also serves as an exit as well as an entrance, and utilising the potential of what we see when we double-back on ourselves, I took the opportunity to create a view where before there was none.

Roses are everywhere in this garden, followed in the season by hydrangeas, all these flowering shrubs nestling seats and spots into their place. Graceful foliage in the shade, fragrance and form in the gentlest of palettes all blurred with perennials and bulbs to join everything together. The seating area has easy, safe steps up to a bench that in itself is a balustrade, beefed up and snuggled into a mass of *Hydrangea arborescens* 'Annabelle'. It's a symbiotic relationship, this one: the hydrangea nestles the bench into security whilst the bench props up floppy Annabelle.

The planting is always everyone's favourite part of the process; it brings with it the sparkle and magic of fairy dust and those all-important iron underpinnings at the same time. Up grow the roses, and up and over they'll continue to grow. In their second summer, they're already looking like they know what to do.

Opposite, above and below. A range of roses, including *Rosa* Desdemona (= 'Auskindling'), *R.* Gentle Hermione (= 'Ausrumba') and *R.* Emily Brontë (= 'Ausearnshaw') thrive in this riverside location.

A Pavilion of Curves

I met Allan McRobie, who teaches engineering at the University of Cambridge, through old friends. Not being the world's greatest mathematician, I didn't think that his book, *The Seduction of Curves*, would succeed in teaching me very much at all, if anything, but how wrong I was. It turns out that geometry and maths have a lot to do with the fact that we find curves, generally speaking, alluring. These smooth, organic lines and surfaces—like those of the human body—appeal to us in an instinctive, visceral way that straight lines, or the perfect shapes concocted by classical geometry, simply don't.

Being completely honest, I'm probably never going to understand the complicated maths behind how and why this resonates so deeply with us. But what I do understand well is when a composition is more than the sum of its parts—how many different elements and forms can work together in a view that sits rather pleasingly with us. Curves are chimeras, they change subtly depending on viewpoint, constantly shape-shifting as we move our own bodies around them. This also is what the very best gardens do, and even my nonmathematical mind realised that we could harness this inherent enchantment within a show garden pavilion, so I set out to create it with Wedgwood at the RHS Chelsea Flower Show in 2018, based in part on McRobie's research. My intention was to harness these theories and embody them in one iconic sculptural shape, then place it within an equally dynamic garden. Transience and an elusive appeal would be key themes.

Months of conversations, studies, sketches, experiments, calculations, and models later, the structure,

The Swallowtail Pavilion in the Wedgwood Garden at the RHS Chelsea Flower Show, 2018, takes a solid material and makes it feel ethereal.

the Swallowtail Pavilion, as Allan named it, took up its place in a garden of its own, celebrating the lines of beauty in nature, the ever-changing curves that are swallowtails, cusps, and folds, creating an engineered, man-made form in a garden where straight lines were few and far between.

Built designs often surprise even the designer; we plan how a garden will look, but we can't anticipate all the special moments concomitant with every bit of sunlight and every breeze. We never take credit for fabulous effects courtesy of Mother Nature. We do appreciate every new shadow, every new glint and glimmer as the garden finds itself and settles in. New displays, new characters, new effects, new feelings. Gardens give and vary every day.

I knew I wanted bronze extruded into a unique but recognizably organic shape, its tensile strength seemingly dependent on thin metal chains strung

between its curved exterior frame. Tested in our minds, the incredible Chelsea team *hoped* that these thousands of filaments would catch the light in an infinite number of ways, forming shadows and veils, bestowing important transparency and translucence, making a filigree of sun. Imagine the sigh of relief when they did just that, setting the way for future structures in future shows.

The romance within a garden is heightened if it unfolds gradually, with each footstep. If you don't quite know what's around the corner, you're enticed to go onwards. Glimpses of more beauty offered through transparent branches, boughs, and plants with open habits all help in this regard, but when it comes to built structures, creating transparency is trickier and often elusive. How to take a solid material and make it feel ethereal rather than clunky?

Opposite and above: Weighty bronze and stone catch a filigree of sunlight; the pavilion's thin metal filaments shimmer subtly as the rays shift gradually along their length.

Left: The simple act of observing how water trickles through a space always has a calming effect on us.

Opposite: Plants featured in the Chelsea show garden include, clockwise from top left, *Laser trilobum, Primula sikkimensis, Geum rivale, Trollius xcultorum* 'Taleggio', and *Iris* 'Carnival Time'.

It's the nature of the material and how it is arranged that can move a clunky imposition into instead a lighter introduction, something which suggests that it is only there if you can see it. Our gaze settling upon just a hint of something, and then registering it and looking at it gives it validity, gives it the right to be there.

To bridge the divide between these sturdy foundations and the filigree web floating above, I crafted springs, tiny waterfalls, streams, and rivulets to run throughout, natural and understated, goals for the whole of the garden. A stream trickles from its source in a boulder and winds its way through the garden; I went back in imaginary time and had the owner of this garden heave a huge found rock in this spot, keeping the carbon footprint as low as possible by using items in situ. I'm also on a one-woman mission to bring back crazy paving and this is just that, on a crazy-large scale, consistent from the tiniest little joint detail through to a massive terrace. To create

cohesion, all the stone—including the rocks and boulders representing furniture—was dragged out of one quarry, brought to the surface, cleaned up a bit, and left alone. Irregular shapes are everywhere in this garden, but still identifiable as "whole" to the eye.

Inspired by the colour trials of Josiah Wedgwood, the planting took its cues from the palest blues, lilacs, lemons, and ambers used by the great ceramist. *Iris pallida* subsp. *pallida* provides a zingy light in this part of the garden—a blue focal point blurring the joins between green and yellow. Early flowering for an iris, it even has a lovely fragrance. A little bit of lemony magic here, a path through woodland there. The twists and turns along these routes make for a meditative journey to a quiet corner carved out of an assembly of rocks and boulders. Water catches the light, and the light sparks the imagination. Calm is achieved by noticing the gentle, constant movement all around. The garden encourages flights of fancy rather than stretches of the imagination.

Quiet Structure

Let's look at what we have here. Not at what is immediately in front of us in the photos overleaf, that charming seductive foreground of plants and pools; I instead to want to focus on what lies beyond the garden. Ancient woodland of oak and beech in a quiet corner of Sussex, hidden away, yet as soon as you step in, you're in an open space—a glade, one could call it. It makes you start to think. You think about the past, what went on in this place; you think about how it's going to work in the future. And how it will work in the present? Well, that happens if the garden takes on a life and a character of its own.

The building gives us clues. A long single storey range of spaces reaching from one side of the house weren't always the store-rooms that they are now—they had been built as sleeping quarters and places of reflection for the nuns who originally lived here. As time passed, marks were made by different people: suppressed during the Dissolution, the house passed into private hands and bits and pieces were added—a wing here, a façade there, a hedge to divide. There's a peaceful sense of something, yet at the same time an overriding feeling that this place has grown into its very best self, as that of a place for a family.

That's what went through my mind as I whiled away the time feeling my way through this garden. What went before—a restorative place of reverence and reflection—and what has come since. People, clatter, fun, noise. I needed to bring the two together. Fun equals play and friends, reflection equals a place to sit by water, restorative equals the goodness of plants.

Campanula and penstemon
are key to creating a romantic, unfussy border against
the façade of this Georgian
house.

Once I have "beaten the bounds" of the place, walked the along the edges of the land and criss-crossed over it, I start to note what is there that I can make use of. How I can divide it up with boundaries between spaces for different uses without making those boundaries too stark? Well, there was already an ornamental fishpond and a big old hedge dividing two large expanses of grass—valuable elements individually, but as a whole the area felt formal and with a sense of the ominous that needed to be firmly steered instead into a sense of welcome.

Even the most formal of gardens can be a real garden for real people. The presence of the heavy old yew hedge offered the idea of a neat enclosing frame near the pool, but it was just too huge; the garden needed to breathe, and so we liberated the hedge by transforming it into a series of individual pillars. They read as a tidy, regimented streak of sentinels, but now the gaps between each dark green upright let the light and the life pass through. Though not a solid wall, it still very effectively divides the garden into visually discrete areas: pool and play to one side, elementally ornamental on the other, devoted to plants.

And so it was that this second area became a place to eat amongst things to eat. Edible and medicinal plants—plants that centuries ago the nuns would have grown and used—spill out from various and numerous beds. The surrounding walls capture the fragrance pushed out by jasmine and many, many roses. Positively smothering this area with looser-form and practical plants helps this area feel cosy and relaxed. As it's just off the kitchen, a potager-themed terrace surrounded by herbs becomes a place of respite in a different way.

Opposite: An existing ornamental pond was the starting point for this area's design concept. The topiary was designed to hide existing drainage covers and to give a feeling of separation between this space and the neighbouring swimming pool.

Above: The layout for this garden was directed by one existing feature: the long rectangular pond. I then layered a series of notional garden rooms around it, each inspired in some way by its neighbour.

A house without climbers in my book is a naked house; these *Trachelospermum jasminoides* are so very happy here and I firmly believe it would have been an absolute travesty not to have planted them. Anchoring new architectural additions to old, and to the ground itself, the scented flowers wiggle their way into the neighbouring roses. In just a few years, this mix of happy climbing plants clad the walls.

We aren't here to impose ourselves on what's already beautiful; instead, it's about knowing when to stop. The existing fishpond and some inconvenient-but-historic drain arrangements were there, and they were there to stay, so their existence dictated the shape of the low hedges of *Ilex crenata*. It was as simple as that. Evaluating with an open mind what can't be changed often gives a massive clue as to what to do with it. And so it was these geometric shapes were formed, almost drawing themselves on the ground plan, their "horizontal-ness" in turn suggesting a need for a foil of tapering, conical topiary that bridges the visual space between the ground plane and the vertical, as if quietly hand-ing over the structure baton to those all-important yew sentinels. Add a bench to sit in and bathe in the green, and the area feels complete.

Big impositions of dark green topiary can say a lot; sometimes too much. They generally feel appropriate against the grandeur of a large historic house, but in other situations they can deliver disappointment by clearly looking out of scale or feeling too formal. Scale, harmony, unity—all these design terms that buzz around do mean something when it comes to choosing that all-important backbone for any gar-den. I would hesitate to create too vast a collection of uniform topiary in the garden of a new house, or in a small garden in the middle of town. Perhaps in a smaller garden a few multi-stemmed large shrubs

An armillary sphere is hugged by English roses including *Rosa* Munstead Wood (= 'Ausbernard'), *R.* Falstaff (= 'Ausverse') and *R.* Young Lycidas (= 'Ausvibrant').

with pretty leaves and even prettier blossom might temper the topiary, linking the garden to its place. A loose lump of pittosporum might provide proportionate framework to that which the holly creates here, or some beech, which, even if manicured into a dome of some sort, still retains a sense of the natural by the very nature of being a native.

Topiary holds the view before allowing the eye to move on. It frames, it engages, and should delight. It does a very good job of guiding our feet from A to B, a kind of filler when you need something simple to join the dots. The Romans knew this; in the first century letter-writer extraordinaire Pliny the Younger noted: "In front of the portico is a sort of terrace, edged with box and shrubs cut into different shapes.

You descend, from the terrace, by an easy slope adorned with the figures of animals in box, facing each other…this is surrounded by a walk enclosed with evergreens, shaped into a variety of forms…the whole is fenced in with a wall completely covered by box cut into steps all the way up to the top."

In this garden, there's another use of topiary which was already existing when I first visited: a dwarf buxus hedge had been planted to edge an existing quatrefoil lined in stone. How long this shape of four overlapping circles had been there, nobody knew; we decided that we may as well keep it. These curves on the ground plan suggested that it needed a central focal point feature with similarly round and classical elements, so we chose an

Opposite: In this swimming pool area, a tapestry hedge with a difference provides privacy and acts as a backdrop to a series of colourful deciduous and evergreen shrubs.

Right and below: Yew sentinels have procumbent roses at their feet for balance, softness, and colour. A series of curved brick and stone steps leads to the play lawn below.

armillary sphere with rings modelling the circles of the celestial sphere. A shake of roses, a fuzz of fennel, perennials in tones of semiprecious stones; tanzanite and bullseye soften the formality and link colours with the Byzantine carnelian and jaspilite featuring on the existing pool paving beyond.

The pool area, bordered by fluffs of roses and tall perennials that blur into the hazy sun of summer adjoins a simple lawn that suggests itself as a play-space simply by its proximity to the swimming area. There's no stark topiary here; everything needed to feel soft, cushiony, playful, so the idea of the stark hedge is rethought. Organisation and manipulation

move away from yew, and instead utilise plants from the woodland background; even copper beech grows up within the hedge itself. It's a Battenberg cake tapestry of hornbeam and copper beech that frames the lawn and continues around the pool for privacy. As simply as that, the three areas are united. The existing overgrown lavender in the hedges at the front of the house were thinned out, given some love, and then scattered throughout the whole garden. They pop up in the new kitchen herb beds, amongst the procumbent roses growing at the foot of the yew columns, and in the generously-sized beds bordering the swimming pool. Nothing should be wasted.

Above, left: This garden room is a pleasant mix of structural and soft, as the *Taxus baccata* topiary is softened by perennials including *Salvia nemorosa* 'Caradonna' and *Verbena bonariensis*. Above, right: *Trachelospermum jasminoides* clothes the stone walls.

Scented plants and herbs
fill the beds in this outdoor
dining area.

Summer Solstice

The writer to whom this garden belongs appreciates unique, exquisite things. Someone willing to add their own magic to it, sprinkle an extra layer of beauty in the form of decorative details on top of the natural beauty offered by the landscape. Here a writer who's a lover of colour, a lover of roses, a lover of variation in forms and tones let loose.

This garden's first iteration was as a show garden. To come up with an idea for an empty space—empty of purpose, empty of people, empty of plants, and yet a space that is to exude character and meaning to everyone eventually ambling by—means the imagination has to work twice as hard. The first step in creation, then, is to conjure up is the person who is going to inhabit the garden. So I talk at length with the garden's "owner" in my mind, thinking of the kinds of details that will suit them perfectly. This one came to me easily; I was lucky because it was the summer solstice when I was first asked to participate in this show.

The long daylight hours of the solstice offer more hours for creativity, making it a ripe time for writers. This writer, perhaps having been taken on a journey by fairies—who knows?—appeared in my mind as a fully formed personality, although interestingly one without gender or physical form.

I continued pondering on writers, and landed on our rich heritage in Britain of writers who have buildings in the garden as dedicated creative spaces. With a lack of an actual place to inspire, the location to needs to be conjured up in the witchcraft of the imagination, and Britain's literary landscape,

For flower show gardens such as this, which begin as empty space—empty of purpose, empty of inhabitants, empty of plants— the designer's imagination has to work twice as hard to plan something with real atmosphere.

Summer Solstice

The summer solstice is a time of strength, joy, and confidence. The longest day. It seems, and it seemed to our ancestors, that the sun stands still in the sky, meaning the sun gods have finally won their battles against the cold and the dark. It's one of the only three nights a year (along with Beltane and Samhain) when spirits go out wandering. According to Celtic folklore, gifted people could join the spirits. It's a time for inspiration, for being led out on that journey into creativity, into a magical place.

Above and right: The conceit for this RHS Chelsea Flower Show garden included a retreat building with a dedicated room for a writer. It was intended as a place of inspiration, a place to retreat to.

therefore, became the inspiration for this place. I wanted to create a sacred hideaway, so that was how it started—the idea of a little nook at the bottom of a garden. Sissinghurst and Vita Sackville-West, Roald Dahl's garden hut, Dylan Thomas's stilted boathouse, Monk's House and Virginia Woolf, Charleston with all its comings and goings: all helped to inform this character and the design. I had to be more specific to give this garden a sense of place in a place without a place, and so it was that I settled on Dorset, and the simplest, most natural place to go for me was the Isle of Purbeck. It's not an actual island but a peninsula place at the end of the world—or so it must have seemed to its neolithic inhabitants, limestone and mudstone cliffs dividing the sea from the barrow-filled hills, which were later to hold the ruins of Corfe Castle, with tumbledown towers and bulging walls that carry the romance of intrigue in every stone.

This Purbeck stone, honey-toned and fossil-filled, combines with English oak to set a warm tone for writing. A two-storey building, with a space to retreat to above and a space to relax below, drops directly into a curving, natural swimming pond, long enough to swim a length, deep enough to take a dive. Water calms the mind as we sit by it, observing whatever decides to make its home here or simply stop by for a temporary float. A chilly plunge in the unheated waters might get the creative juices flowing again, a good spot for chasing away moments of procrastination.

The word "retreat" is often used in garden design to describe a desire for a place with a contemplative atmosphere, and in this retreat garden there's also a retreat within a retreat. The upper level of the building, reached by a ship's ladder and drawbridge-style trapdoor, is the place where the action happens.

When the trapdoor is closed, you're secreted away. Separated from everything with just the sounds of the garden for company. But at the same time, you can't escape being a part of the garden—those sounds tie you to it, a round peephole window letting you see more at your discretion. Having

Opposite: The textured bark of the majestic, multistemmed *Betula nigra* inspired the colour palette for the surrounding plantings; deep reds and wine shades complement its browns and maroons.

Right, top: An oak walkway leading to the retreat runs over the water. Right, bottom: Silver foliage adds bright highlights to the perennial planting.

reached the top, the only way out is down, but the writer wants to linger.

This window flirts with being a threshold to nudge inspiration into the imagination. Thresholds contain mystery, not only by offering a suggestion of where we might be going—a liminal point frames that perception, suggesting an atmosphere of possibility before we even traverse it. When you're up here, *you're* the secret, with the very special luxury of a secret glimpse out onto the colours and textures that go towards creating the feeling that this is a place that will stand the test of time, even if the reality is that just a few weeks later this garden will be carefully taken to pieces and rebuilt in a place where it will live on.

All these things and more, I'm looking at and considering when deep within the task of creating a colour scheme for every garden. Every garden has a different palette, some similar, yes, but never the same. Here, the elegant multistems of *Betula nigra*, a tree by its very nature at home by the water, has its bark as an absolute jewel, the crumbling flaking textures with pinks and browns giving a cue as to which roses will work as near-ish neighbours. For this writer is in my mind a lover of colour, a lover of roses, a lover of forms and tones let loose, so roses 'Chianti' and 'Tuscany Superb' team up with

a standard wisteria and a touch of the unusual, *Westringia fruticosa* trapping the light with its gentle spikes of silver foliage.

The flowerbeds themselves direct us to more mystery, winding and circling with offshoots into other places of retreat. Large rough-hewn boulders with one of their sides sawn and polished to glass to reveal their strata, their layers of time bringing us right back into the present with this sheen of a finish which owes its existence to modern machinery. An encircled seating area showcases another arrangement of this same stone its more natural form.

Above, left: Water-loving plantings line the swimming pond's filtration area. Above, right: *Rosa* 'Louise Odier' and *Chaerophyllum hirsutum* 'Roseum'. Opposite: A circle of polished pieces of Purbeck stone creates a seating area almost completely enveloped by flowers.

The artist Tom Stogdon, when introduced to the garden's materials and notion of time, was immediately drawn to that most familiar of fossil forms, the ammonite, and took it as a loose shape for balancing stones in a way that creates something new of something old to form a focal point. Beauty in its calm solidity, this sculpture took up its place in the space, becoming so much more than just a decorative feature. Its form was, as intended, the beginning, or perhaps the end, of an ammonite, curves which followed the curves of the paths leading in and out and around of the different nooks and crannies of seats and moments of pause that all go towards making up a garden. A link between tall building and low benches, this stone tail-end began to form a function of its own as, on placement of the final stone, it became a kind of a porthole in its echoes of the window above, another window giving onto different scenes within the garden and another almost-liminal space out into the rest of the busy showground, so near and yet seemingly worlds away from this space away.

A happy accident is a beautiful event, although I wonder whether it was entirely an accident. Sometimes things are meant to be: a garden with true atmosphere is the result of the rich creativity of so many wandering imaginations coming together over the years, with an intervention here and an edit there, original thought and experiments and trials of ideas. To capture in a show garden this temporary image, even though a part of many processes, is what I dream of, and sometimes that imaginary resident seems to come to life. One did here, choosing and placing this sculpture by an invisible hand, leaving it to enjoy for those who follow.

Seeing the Vision

In the heart of the Wealden countryside, halfway between the iconic gardens of Sissinghurst and Great Dixter, parts of this beautiful landscape have been brought into daily use over a decade, homage to these long-lived precedents. Autumn is approaching, but even as grey skies start to envelop us there are still colours of late-flowering perennials to revel in, so, spurred on by their presence we defy the shortening days by taking furtive last splashes in the pool.

To help this ancient farmhouse live its best life during its current occupants' tenancy rather than trying to create a replica of what might have come before, however, I followed my own prescription of not interfering with the landscape beyond, respecting what brilliant Mother Nature does best, and at the same time gently intervening by placing contemporary elements informed by context. Sloping banks of lavender were here when I first arrived; these gave up their place to new terraces full of textures and colours in a palette requested by the owners, inspired directly by their love of the nearby gardens at Great Dixter.

There are intuitive ways through this garden, the landscape that sits around a farmhouse. The explanation of how we arrived at the path that the main journey follows starts with the existing beeches and oaks, here for so long that some of their fallen companions now even form part of the buildings themselves. A drover's lane goes right through all, and the shapes and contours of the land provided the hints as to how we could make use of the different areas and give them meaning and purpose even centuries after cattle had ceased to tread here. For example,

This swimming pool is a recent arrival in an ancient place—ensuring that it sits well in its location was the key to pleasing the genius loci.

Above: Ornamental grasses and late-summer perennials including *Helenium* 'Waltraut' and *Rudbeckia fulgida* var. *deamii* create a soft screen to bridge a change in ground levels. Right: *Helenium* 'Waltraut'.

this seventeenth-century drover's lane transformed smoothly into a twenty-first century drive, a hollow becomes a tucked-away outdoor kitchen, a barn once used for farming becomes a space for a different kind of work and a new place to play—a home office and location for the very best of parties. Gradually, if you sit and contemplate different areas, their purpose, the point of their existence, will reveal themselves. At the same time, their history makes itself felt too. I can't tell you exactly who it is nudging me forward, but there's very definitely a guiding presence, urging me and encouraging me, and reminding me not to go too far. I know what I'm allowed to do, and I know what's too much. The spirits of the garden keep me in check.

Stretches of plantings with the splaying bright green falls of *Euphorbia* x *pasteurii*, the offspring of *E. stygiana* and *E. mellifera*, capture fractals and make patchwork patterns against the neighbouring plants. Turn a corner, and a pair of beds are our companions down to a more wooded area where cornus stems light up the winter dullness, their leaves in summer disappearing into an undemanding layer of green. The journey takes us along and down through twin *Betula utilis* var. *jacquemontii*, silver trunks that read as ghostly or cheering, depending on the light. On we go around, through shrub beds in shades of green and purples, a colourway chosen to work with (rather than to stand out from) the ancient beeches and oaks, and to work with the materials of the house.

In a dip created by the removal of a barren shrubbery, we come to an outdoor kitchen that flanks part of an entertaining area. This space of course couldn't ever be designed to look as if it had always been there, but with careful study of contours and surroundings, we managed to snuggle it into a spot linking a party room with the main terrace without making it the central feature of the garden. We go past here and over a terrace to a swimming pool, another new arrival in this old, old place.

The creation of a garden is ideally about a lifetime-long conversation with its custodian. Together, we watch over how it develops, we tweak plans as nature shows us a better way, we take comfort in the trees and plants that grow here and the birds who visit. I work with the contours of the land, celebrating the situation and trying to avoid too much hard intervention in terms of paving, too much obvious "design." Less is more and we must remember that in the end, the land gives us all the beauty we need.

Opposite: An outdoor kitchen and large entertaining area now sit in a dip created by the removal of a barren shrubbery.

Above, top: Late-summer perennials create foreground interest while a birch avenue beyond provides a backdrop of subtle structure.

Above, left: *Persicaria amplexicaulis* 'Firetail', *Foeniculum vulgare* 'Giant Bronze', and *Verbena bonariensis*. Above, right: *Gladiolus* 'Ruby'.

Overleaf: Less is more. Leaving some open, uncultivated space allows us to appreciate the land's natural beauty.

Samhain

One of the four fire festivals in ancient Celtic tradition, Samhain marks another changing of the seasons. In this tradition, the year was divided into light and darkness: Beltane was the light, whilst Samhain represented the dark half of the year. These two halves were further divided by the festivals of Imbolc and Lughnasadh. We might be surprised to learn that, though we might not call it by the same name, we're already familiar with Samhain—Hallowe'en is believed to be a descendant.

This was once one of the most important festivals of the year, a time when the world of the gods made itself visible to man, and where only offerings and sacrifices were going to keep you out of trouble. As a kind of a new year, it was a time when the harvest had been gathered and preparations were made for the year to come. Animals were brought in for the winter, feasts were held, and matters of business were sorted out. The seventeenth-century Irish historian Geoffrey Keating wrote in *The History of Ireland* that "it was their custom to assemble on the eve of Samhain to offer sacrifice to all the gods…it was of obligation under penalty of fine to quench the fires of Ireland on that night, and the men of Ireland were forbidden to kindle fires except from [the main] fire." This Samhain fire was kindled by the bones of the animal sacrifices. And so this "bone fire" became our bonfire.

A new take on traditional shrubbery; ornamental grasses combine with physocarpus, hydrangea, and acers to add an unimposing weight in the part of the garden farthest from the house.

Pub Garden

People make gardens into gardens. One way or another any patch or sprawl of land that has been tamed to least some extent reveals our presence. We do see ourselves as the custodians of places, guardians who have a responsibility for the health of an area borrowed from nature for a while. And we create gardens so that we can use them, be out there amongst plants, and when a garden is also a public space, the question "Who is the garden really for?" becomes a very big question indeed.

For as long as forever, fire has drawn everyone to it. The Latin word for fireplace, or hearth, is *focus*, no accident it's come to mean something we want to look at, to gather round. The focal point. For this garden of many functions, for many different people, a central fire was conceived as an element to bring people together. It's a pub garden, yes, meaning a space for music performances, weddings, Frost Fairs, Cuckoo Fairs, creative workshops, as well as a place to eat, have a drink, sit and read, gather with friends. Being public, it also needs to function all year round, and it needs to provide a brilliant backdrop for special events in people's lives. Fire was one strong feature to help accomplish all these things.

This village public house planned four Hobbit-style guest lodges with wonky doorways nestled into the landscape, slightly sunken so as not to dominate the skyline, and the garden is intended to wind round them. With the architecture leaning towards something magical and little bit mystical, thoughts turned to the labyrinth at Glastonbury Tor and the idea of paths leading to somewhere but the journey itself being as important as the destination. The garden visitor weaves in and around, travelling through spots hidden by planting. The space isn't huge, so these quirky new

rooms, each with an interior unique from the others, needed a space filled with character on the outside too. Privacy is key: privacy from the other lodges, from the pub, and also from the neighbouring car park.

Layers and contours, ups and downs, helped achieve that in a way that feels organic. Height changes can deliver points of unexpected interest, a unique circulation pattern, a bit of pause. Paths clearly lead to *somewhere*, but the journey itself is made as important as the destination.

Up until this stage in the design I've imagined an atmosphere, where all these elements are, and how they will all come together, how it's going to feel to be in the garden, how it's going to make people feel when they look at it. But the fact is that I don't know what the space is actually going to *look like* until that layout is complete. I've got a pretty good idea, but at this stage the client is still bearing with me on this leap of faith that they've taken, hanging on to that idea that they and I have discussed of what this garden is going to be. As soon as I know that it works in terms of atmosphere, elements, routes and feel, then that's the moment. That's when I know what it's going to look like.

That is the stage when I can really start to get this planting going; just before I do this, I take a step back and remind myself what this whole space is *for*. Like editing a book, I usually take something out—maybe there's a frill too many, perhaps I'm focusing too much on the individual areas. This is the point at which I remind myself that all these smaller areas are intended to work together as a pub garden—a place for one, a place for many. So seating is needed: a circular palisade of weathered timbers creates a seating area with a firepit, forming a central space large enough to host events.

Left: The journey is as important as the destination, a cosy firepit, in the garden at The Bell in Ticehurst. Overleaf: Bands of *Calamagrostis* x *acutiflora* 'Karl Foerster' bring height and structure to this pub garden, and catch the sun as it sets.

And the space needed to work for a variety of events including weddings, music festivals, and fairs, whilst local artists display changing artwork here and there.

To avoid stumbles and trips at points where levels change, a show of beautiful but deterring prickly plants often do the trick: enter thorny *Rosa spinosissima* and also *R. rugosa*. Perfectly invasive, the latter will spread conveniently through this contained space.

Plants can of course also add privacy while acting as soft-but-effectual screens. Here, a mix of flowers and grasses offer absolutely uplifting make-you-feel-good positive pops of colour throughout the year, all bounded by edible hedging and fruit trees whose bounty is destined for the pub kitchen. All useful and familiar edibles: serviceberry, quince, hazel, Szechuan pepper, blackthorn, plum, pear, autumn olive, plus roses for harvesting petals and hips. Plenty of bounty for foraging cooks, plenty of food for the birds.

To keep the space feeling approachable and rustic, gabion walls edge the garden. These are given an unusual dose of personality by including items beyond rocks: we added objects that found their way from the kitchen, such as empty bottles with lids on, broken crockery, beautiful things that have served their first purpose and now find another.

Backdrop sorted, privacy comes back into mind. We need veils here and there, and we also need to guide the visitor along and through this garden; the upright

Opposite, left: The client already owned the olive in front of this edible hedge; it now sits with apple and pear trees. Dahlias carry colour through the autumn.

Opposite, right: Drought-tolerant *Erigeron karvinskianus* lives happily on top of stone gabion walls.

Right: In spring, a meadow of tulips and other spring bulbs creates an ever-changing display as well as a floral accompaniment to wedding photographs, popular here.

Overleaf: *Dahlia* 'Ambition' and *D.* 'Dark Spirit' feature boldly against the earthy tones of grass *Molinia caerulea* subsp. *arundinacea* 'Transparent'.

stems of *Calamagrostis* x *acutiflora* 'Karl Foerster' are just the thing for this. Semi-see-through when viewed as a whole, this ornamental feather grass performs well as a straight-backed stealthy sentry, forming landmarks to suggest the way. At a lower level, mounds of rosemary form loose evergreen shapes as a contrast to the tall grass, and lavender's grey foliage lasts long after its scent has finally gone for the season.

Structure complete, it's time for the pretties. Whilst the actual planting design is one of the very last things to be decided, I turn over options in my mind from the beginning. What'll look good in April? Tulips, of course—a meadow of bulbs. Then come *Erigeron karvinskianus* and hardy geraniums

for an easy, low-maintenance May and June, sedum for chunky structure, *Stipa tenuissima* for grassy lowlights against their taller grassy cousins, scabious and ox-eye daisies for the pollinators, as well as for any brides. The planting needs to be soft, to work with what surrounds it, to be able to live without much soil to speak of, to blend in, to make welcoming what are clearly barriers, all without looking too planned. People have fun here, and hopefully remember special days in a place filled with bees and butterflies. The stepped beds filled with colour have led to the management needing to ask pottering people not to frolic in flowerbeds on a regular basis. I'll take it as a compliment, though.

Making a Garden with an Architect

Every site offers some design direction to us, whether it's the house, the way people live in the house, the view from the house out to the garden, or the view from the garden out over the rolling land-scape beyond. Sometimes, we think we're fortunate enough to have all these fortunes overlap, as here: rooms with a view, in a garden with a view. The potential is huge and the possibilities endless.

This conundrum is a common one. How to narrow down a seemingly infinite number of good solutions? In design school, you're often taught to pin down the Big Idea, a theme to help you create a cradle for your thoughts. Once we get out there into the world and work with real people in real gardens, however, this Big Idea often dissolves into what is essentially a silent, most gentle interrogation of who and what we are working with.

So when an architect is involved, there is an even more exciting layer of opportunity—the chance to talk with the creator of the building, who will have had their own insights about context and space and light. They had their own Big Idea, they have studied the land and got to grips with its physical demands. They've devoted months or years to making some-thing solid here; when it comes to adding the exterior softness that can make a house a welcoming home, they generously hand over to the landscape designer, and that's when a really substantial, delving-deep conversation can take place. When design minds meet in terms of philosophy, a result that will seem like spontaneous serendipity to all who view the com-bined creation later often ensues.

In this landscape, the straight lines and hedges marking out the more formal garden areas near the house are intended as a statement of intent, of civilisation.

A good place to retreat to, this house is an elegant marriage of sixteenth-century and Victorian elements, punctuated with sympathetic contemporary additions. The landscape was a collaboration with nature, the gardens a collaboration with us all. Here, Mother Nature is let well and truly off the leash—the form of the surrounding land takes us quickly away from the formal lines set out by the architect near the house. To echo this, clipped topiary and hedges have their place up high, near the building, and then gradually dissipate and fade into meadow as order passes the baton to wildness.

In this landscape, the straight lines marking out the areas near the house are a statement of intent, of civilisation. A bold, brave arrangement of rectilinear beds, grass terraces, and chunky slab steps hold the house to the land and announce that the humans who have been occupying this site for five centuries intend to stay. These are the results of the initial collaboration between the architect, William Deakins, and the owner. Stability to match the august history of the original house was wanted, so along came strong mounds of yew and lengths of beech. They define and say very clearly how this garden should be negotiated. It's a decisive arrangement for the part of the garden that people would use the most due to its proximity to the rooms inside. To ease the transition from, in essence, hard materials to soft countryside, we wanted an atmosphere that smudges borders and tumbles gently into the Sussex landscape.

Opposite: Simple mown paths create appealing routes through long grasses.

Above: Large slabs of granite set into slopes to create stairs echo the warm tones of the house's exterior walls.

Though they don't have walls of half timber, the new areas outside form a series of no less distinct rooms, and there as on interiors, steps get us from A to B, from one level to another. As we change level, change "room," our intent for using that space changes outdoors as well. Big brave slabs of granite set into slopes echo the warm tones of the house's exterior walls, seamlessly providing a foothold as we ease ourselves into softer surroundings; they're easy on the eye and point us squarely in the direction of relaxation. The lines of these steps fade in and out of the land, the materials appearing and disappearing in and out of mind, in and out of view. Tall perennials create the fizz and fluff to balance the Tudor geometry, and all create a series of changing scenes as seasons move from one into the next. Timeless.

Opposite, above and below: Tall spires of veronicastrum bring subtle colour, height, and texture to the terraced beds with their boundaries of beech and yew as they negotiate the contours of the site.

Above: The client requested a subtle planting palette that would sit comfortably in front of this historic timber-framed building.

A Barn for All Seasons

When the light is at its most fleeting and everything has stopped, it's winter solstice. A time to balance out the exuberance of the summer equinox, a time when the garden seems to sleep. This garden stops me in my tracks every time I visit in the cold season. Intended to display rich colour even when branches are bare, layers of time also show through—the bleached bones themselves are perceptible, laid bare. Pure structure, taking centre stage, denuded of all that dresses it in warmer months.

When confronted with a place or landscape steeped in history, I take into consideration what it's been about in the past, what it's trying to be now, the location, the position, who's next door. What I feel obliged to celebrate versus what details I actually want to celebrate. Here it's oak trees, fields. The place. What do I want to make of it? A setting, a journey round a garden and a journey though time. Although the latter is not necessarily easy to articulate, it's what weighs on me as I stand in such a beautiful location and try to build up my nerve, convince myself I have any right to meddle and interfere. Gradually, a picture of possibilities forms in my mind. What can I add? Intimacy and corners and destinations, defined retreats and places opening up as if accidentally onto wilder views. Secret spots and open places.

That is how this garden happened. The owners identified a place to develop a secret walled garden of their very own. The rest was dictated by the land and by the house and its history. Acting as a plant diviner, I set about beating the bounds and getting a feel for the property. And it taught me a

lesson, gently guiding me towards what it wanted. Centuries earlier, this barn wouldn't have been edged by a garden, but it would have had lines of desire and habit leading to it—drover lines, cart lines. It was a place that people come to regularly; it was a barn with a purpose. And so this barn attracts people again now, if nestled away behind a new line of plantings.

Winter bones emerge frozen, stark, yet animated in a field where there is seemingly nothing else going on. That it looks complete, quiet, and established was the point—for much had gone on here just a short time before. The eighteenth-century barn had actually been picked up, moved from its original location twenty miles away, and painstakingly rebuilt here, beam by beam, peg by peg, tile by tile. A new place for an old building, a building that needed a new incarnation to feel like a home, a place to anchor it to unfamiliar land, to give it permanence.

An empty field is full of potential. Within any framework, bare or crowded, I search for stories. A way to reinterpret history for the now, to give a place some meaning. And what better literal framework is there than a walled garden, one full of rambling roses and hung with wisteria and clematis, around simply divided beds as a classic and effective announcement of refinement, careful attention, and intent? Benches placed at key points provide satisfyingly secluded places to read, to shelter from the sun, to enjoy the fragrance of the scented plants in summer. Paths through wildflower meadows lead to a hornbeam cloister on the other side of the

Within any framework, bare or not, it's possible to create stories, meaning, texture.

garden—another room—but this time with walls of green, enclosing a still pool designed to capture the reflections of a steady oak nearby and the shifting skies overhead.

Smaller rectangles of reflection in the form of water tanks pick up the skies elsewhere in the garden; hidden behind hedges, they sit just outside a music room most often occupied by this home's pianist. Bird feeders are everywhere, providing seed at a barren time of year. In this former void, the new routes lead us actively to moments imbued with emotion, reinforcing the worth of taking a journey.

Winter reveals the denouement of this story's plot. Green trees silver over, life hides away beneath ground and under cloud, and the days are chill and still. We feel dread, perhaps, at the knowledge that

the longest night of the year marches to us in an unavoidable approach, a niggling discomfort at the certainty of impending darkness that we know will drag on for months. But the acceptance of the constant cycle of the seasons also brings some comfort; we find it in our best selves to step out and experience frost, let its sharp presence equally reassure us that nature operates on a schedule so predictable our ancestors could time their sowing and rituals and harvests to it, organise their entire lives around it. So why shouldn't we feel as comfortable walking among long shadows cast by short days as in blazing overhead sun? They say change is the only constant; perhaps, but that statement feels like a misinterpretation by people who are too removed from the cycles of nature to recognize the wholly predictable pattern repeated yearly by time itself.

Opposite: A sort of cloister of pleached hornbeam frames a reflecting pool.

Above, top: Low beech and hornbeam hedges define a side garden and pick up the colours of the pleached hornbeam beyond.

Above, bottom: A frosty sculpture in the walled garden seems like a ghostly nod to the year to come.

Left: Hard and soft mingle together to create structure and interest in the winter light.

Opposite, top: For as long as they remain upright, ornamental grasses are left standing to provide habitat and food in this garden for wildlife.

Opposite, bottom: Even in the bitter cold, some roses continue to push out a hopeful flower, whilst crab apples provide welcome hits of winter colour.

Blossom in Frost

Why is it that we are so often taken by surprise when a late frost settles in? We think of Jack Frost as a silvery, wintry character, but he often visits just at that very moment when we've decided to place him firmly out of our minds. Our perennial optimism leads to expected surprise when he appears in April, and even more surprise—verging on horror—in May if we wake in the morning and have a sneaking feeling that a certain someone has had a bit of a dance around the garden overnight, then confirm our suspicions by looking out of the window to see the grass glittering wickedly around early bulbs and punctual blossoms. No wonder they call those early warm days a Fool's Spring.

This garden has been liberated by its custodians, who removed dead and diseased trees and undertook an energetic replanting with a determination to give back to the land. Cherries and serviceberries now stand by, creating a bit of early spring cheer as the only architecture needed here alongside dollops of *Osmanthus* x *burkwoodii* that circle a roundabout placed to create a sense of arrival whilst at the same time maintaining openness and light.

Scrubby functional slopes held the land back; a transformation with wildflower seeding has turned them into banks of welcome, with *Narcissus pseudonarcissus* and camassia naturalising in the poor soil. Thresholds are temporarily framed by tulips, planted in place for one season before being moved to the surrounding meadows in the hope that they may flower again in the future.

Pinks and whites are at branch height everywhere and delight us, as is the way with blossom.

Spring blossoms now bring welcome early cheer to formerly-neglected banks in this Sussex garden.

Above and right: A view
though blossoming cherries
and amelanchiers to a circle
of *Osmanthus* x *burkwoodii*
creates a sense of arrival
whilst at the same time maintaining openness and light.

Above: Spring bulbs including tulips, muscari, and ipheion provide colour along the ground; higher up, early flowering clematis add interest before the roses onto which they are trained begin to bloom.

The delicate steadfastness of small blooms, pastels and tissues, is at odds with the icy temperatures as they try to defy the season. The magnolia, though bolder in form, is the one that makes us most nervous as each year we send up a little wish to any nearby garden spirits as we witness the slow splitting open of its buds, whose toughness has protected them thus far. It's a garden prayer, and most gardeners would be willing to bargain something very precious that the flower petals remain untouched by that mischievous, steely visitor.

Sometimes we're rewarded; other times no one seems to have heard. Lucky one year, not so lucky the next. That's how gardening often goes. As soon as we accept that, gardening makes much more sense, as otherwise it's tough to keep on persevering, year after year, in the knowledge that something may be taken away from us on a weathery whim. Yes, the frost may turn petal pinks into a smudgy, sludgy mess of brown, but we may well have been lucky enough to catch the petals out in bloom for at least a day, basking in the romance of it all. The sight of the beauty is enough to keep us grateful, to uphold our commitment to the garden for what it plans to provide as the wheel of the year turns.

Above, left and right: The garden already featured some beautiful magnolias, whose romantic highlights of colour set the pastel tone for the rest of the planting.

Overleaf: Topiary mounds punctuate the lawn's threshold, providing a gentle intervention to demarcate the line between heavily cultivated areas and the landscape beyond.

Spring Equinox

At the spring equinox, the length of the day finally equals the length of the night. New hope is breathed in, as we feel any or all of the sun gods— Osiris, Dionysus, Hun Hunahpu—are out there, battling darkness on our behalf and winning. As the struggle continues, the seeds and bulbs wait in the soil, just beneath the earth's surface, ready to pop through when the battle is won. For they know more about these cycles than we do. Spring will come, one day. In those first weeks when the calendar tells us it's approaching, even when it remains resolutely cold, I dare you to open your doors and windows and drink in the sounds. The birds are busier, and there's just enough blue in the sky for a sailor's waistcoat.

It isn't hard to invoke the goddess of spring as you wander round this garden in Norfolk, where as new life is breathed in, the orchids have returned to grow. I know that Eostre's hares are seen in this garden: associated with magic, shape-shifting, intuition and rebirth, hares were once thought to lay eggs. They appear here around the time of the spring equinox, boxing in the fields and acting as a sign of a fruitful year ahead. This is a place of hope and productive ideas as well as fruit and flowers.

Birds too offer us signs to the meaning of the place. The Druids tell that the blackbird is the way between each season and represents the new, whilst the wise owl is seen often at twilight here— the fairy hour—as spirits and witches start to go about their business. Ravens fly overhead and bring with them the representation of protection

This Norfolk home belongs to the writer Justine Picardie and her husband, Philip Astor.

Spring Has Always Been Celebrated

Druids celebrate the spring equinox with the ceremony of Alban Eilir, the "light of the earth." Eostre, the Anglo-Saxon goddess of fertility for humans and crops, is also fêted in spring with her symbols, the egg and the hare. The Welsh flower maiden Blodeuwedd was created from spring oak flowers, broom flowers, and meadowsweet, but then was turned into an owl as a punishment for plotting to kill her husband. This was the ultimate penalty as it meant she could never show her face in daylight again. Spring is a time for joyful celebration: the Jewish festival of Purim carries with it much merrymaking, whilst in India, the Hindu festival of Holi celebrates the arrival of spring, love, and fertility, celebrated by explosions of coloured powder that people throw at one another.

Romantic and natural, with a real sense of place and to whom it belongs, this garden emanates feelings of magic and friendship. Simplicity is all in this beautiful, serene garden.

as they do so, whilst nearby swans, the poet's birds, move along the River Waveney. The birds of inspiration, they draw up creativity from other worlds into ours, reminding us to dig deep and channel inner feelings.

I have spent special, perfect days with the writer Justine Picardie walking around the gardens she and her husband, Philip, been encouraging, studying the landscape that surrounds the house as we plot new and ever gentle interventions. The meadows we planned and planted now flourish under Justine's care, a succession of spring and early summer bulbs gradually giving

way to the native wildflowers, little dots of colour against the green positively humming and buzzing with pollinators.

Wildflower meadows are habitats beyond a value that I can assign to them. We added a few non-natives, as a diversity of plants extends the seasons in terms of providing pollen and habitat. A succession of snowdrops and dwarf irises, wild daffodils and snakeshead fritillaries precede the wildflowers and grasses seen here. Then it's time for camassia and allium to sparkle blues and violets just before the ragged robins and ox-eye daisies. Little jewels dotted throughout: a flowery mead.

Above: Wildflower meadows are habitats almost beyond value, they support so many species throughout the year.

Opposite: Soft, romantic planting creates the gentlest kind of transition from terrace to lawn.

You don't always need to landscape the whole of your garden in order to make a difference. Often, a thought-through planting is enough to change everything. A charming side door at the house was made into something special by a carefully considered selection of plants. Romantic and natural, with a real sense of where it is and to whom it belongs, this garden is full of feelings of magic and friendship. The plants also carry mystery and history. *Tricyrtis formosana* 'Dark Beauty', otherwise known as the toad lily, is perfect for a shady border and utterly secure in her beauty, but best appreciated close up, so is often overlooked. For Justine I wanted the entrance to feel serenely beautiful rather than jump out at you as you approach. It stands quietly, awaiting your arrival in your own good time.

Later in the summer, scented roses become armfuls of fragrance and beauty and hope, calling to mind a farm of roses in the south of France, dedicated to creating the most beautiful of fragrances. In her books, Justine brings to us the courageous spirits of her sister Ruth, the designer Coco Chanel, and the flower farmer Catherine Dior; this garden bears witness to inspiration and memory, to the telling of stories that are so much more than paintings of words. The spirits of these people, now gone but still very much here, are inextricably linked with this peaceful place.

Is it just me, or do you sense them too?

Above, top and above: The geometric forms of camassia and allium sparkle in shades of blue and violet against a backdrop of green.

Opposite: A charming side door at the house now truly beckons with plants chosen for their delicacy and lightness.

Rising Energy

Any thoughts of grey skies are banished as you step into this garden full of energy. This flower-filled, maxi-textured, multicoloured, happiness-bringing garden belonging to the hairstylist Sam McKnight never fails to put a pep in one's step. Zigzagging along the garden, you also zigzag back in time: the simplest of winter structure shows bare bones and curving ways which suggest both a journey and a hint of things to come. The energy and hope naturally entwined with the beginning of May are prefaced by thousands of tulips, an education in the possibilities of colour taught to me over the years by this dear friend. Roses, whose gentle tones feel quiet in contrast to the preceding tulips, are followed by an extravaganza of colour from a dahlia explosion, surprising and at the same time completely fitting, the last high peak of colour in the growing season.

This garden belongs to a true lover of plants. Too unassuming to call himself a plantsman, even though he is, Sam will confess to being a planta-holic. Many is the time we've looked at the garden and said out loud, "There is no more room for more plants!" and yet an hour or so later, we start to egg each other on, seeking permission for an addition we both know is inevitable. Plants simply want to come here.

This garden's simple patch of lawn was once a lot bigger, taking up the whole garden in fact. In the revised design's first iteration, snaking eights of flowerbeds curved along both edges of the grass, with a central island bed set in to create a soft division, which creates the idea that there might

This flower-filled garden belonging to hairstylist Sam McKnight never fails to bring a smile for its sheer exuberance.

Beltane

The Gaelic May Day festival, Beltane, marks a time when we start to feel that we are truly able to achieve things, when we can turn on creative energy and accomplish things that we've only been thinking about doing in the grey days of winter and early spring. It marks the midway point between the spring equinox and summer solstice, and was traditionally commemorated by the lighting of a huge bonfire.

Thoughts turn from introspection to appreciation of what's around us again as the world turns fertile, cattle can safely be put back out to green pastures, and the living world starts to unravel its magic. We feel connected to it, and individual hearth fires would have been extinguished and re-lit from one communal fire to literally rekindle connection between neighbours as the world passes from darkness into full light. There's a sense of wonder and hope at Beltane, as we rediscover ways to engage with the land.

As time passes, the lawn inevitably shrinks and the flowerbeds grow ever larger; more specimens are constantly added to this plantsman's paradise.

be something beyond what you can see, if only you were to go a little bit closer to find out. The initial idea was that there should be enough room for picnic teas on the grass, plenty of space for friends to feel at ease and sprawl.

However, as the plants have taken up their positions in the beds and made in their display a very strong case for their existence, becoming friends themselves, the grassed area has gradually grown smaller and the borders stealthily larger, each year nibbling into the lawn more and more. But people adapt to the space; they move around and pause where it feels right. And there are many comfortable spots. For tea, for talking about gardens, for finding out about plants. I wonder how many people have

got the gardening bug after visiting here. Gardening with friends is, after all, the dream.

At Beltane, the garden transmits feelings of new light and new life. Gentle pinks and deep reds are joined but never interrupted by oranges and apricots; pastels seem at home here and it's hard to imagine it having any other atmosphere. Yet later in the year, these soft colours give much of their space over to the colours of fire as dahlias and gladioli turn the garden from soft to strong, a new type of energy as the wheel of the year continues to turn. Here in Sam's garden, the scene is set and the place is made. How many plants have been added over the years? I've lost count, but they always make themselves at home in this magical, happiest of gardens.

Opposite: These maximalist flowerbeds are themselves the garden's architecture; they create a series of masses which at once define and conceal.

Above: Between us, Sam and I have lost count of the number of roses in this garden devoted to their beauty. They include *Rosa* Lady of Shalott (= 'Ausnyson'), *R.* Gentle Hermione (= 'Ausrumba'), and *R.* Gertrude Jekyll (= 'Ausbord').

A Garden of Neighbours

When the summer properly starts, it's time to look at what we have grown well in our gardens, and also time to evaluate how our year is going. The long stretch of holiday weeks was designed so children could help with the harvest. It's historically a time of coming together, of neighbours and families pitching in, and in this series of three gardens, each next door to the other, there's an element of collaboration in how different households might come together today to create spaces for people and for wildlife, with neither taking precedent over the other.

The first in this terrace of neighbouring gardens is a wildlife garden, matching a traditional expectation of what a wildlife garden might look like: nothing too glamorous or new or gleaming, scattered piles of logs and buckets of water. It belongs to a person finding it a little harder to get around, someone who's perhaps a bit older, who maybe hasn't as much energy to keep the garden super pristine, who loves plants for their individual forms, who takes pride in vegetable-growing, and most importantly, who loves nature and wildlife.

A range of flower shapes is important, whatever your preferred garden style; different species head for different flowers, so provide a smorgasbord of opportunities. As far as roses are concerned, a big, open flower is best for pollinators to swoop right into. Fennel, fleabane, foxgloves, chives, mint: they've all found their way to this spot. You do have to climb through to get in, but it's lovely once you're on the inside. I'm guessing lots of us have a spot like this somewhere in the garden, where we can let it all hang out and not be constantly controlling it. Open

The range of different flower shapes in this wildlife garden is intended to offer a smorgasbord of opportunities for visiting pollinators.

boundaries allow hedgehogs to tootle through, and there's water and shelter and food.

This show garden (RHS Hampton Court Flower Show, 2019) did cause a stir for a specific reason. The central garden features a clover lawn, and that was the first time a lawn alternative to a manicured patch of velvety green had been presented. Heaven for pollinators, a clover lawn is obviously not a barefoot playground, but with stepping stones and judicious inclusion of nearby paths, these can be fabulous. I'm not saying no to lawn; soft short grass is still useful for play, leisure, and short-beaked birds (and dogs) whilst the clover is in flower. But for a bee paradise and a visual green treat in July, you can't do better.

This was envisioned as a space enjoyed by a young family, whilst next door to *them*, a younger couple enjoyed something simpler, cheaper, more in keeping with the way they live: time-poor but who still want their garden to be a haven for wildlife. All these imaginary people all have their own individualised gardens tailored to their specific time-of-life needs, yet share in the common pursuit of providing food, shelter,

and water for wildlife. Wildflower areas are so easy to maintain—a cut once or maybe twice a year and that's it, honestly. To zhoosh them up, I introduce here and there perennials that I know will stand an excellent chance of survival amongst the wildflowers: *Echinacea pallida* and *Verbena officinalis* var. *grandiflora* 'Bampton' survive well in such a position, unsurprising when you think how happily they multiply when left to their own devices. And a reminder that there doesn't need to be just one designated dining space in the garden—using fewer hard materials is better for the environment, and avoiding expense is better for us all. No imposition of a flagstone terrace is necessary. Just a sprinkling of inspiration and a scattering of imagination—pull up a chair into the wildflower meadow and quietly watch nature at its busiest. Everyone's happy: the garden owner, the birds, insects, and mammals. Job done. Whichever way you approach it, choosing this "less is more" approach is a rewarding pursuit. Make the garden, tend the garden lightly, enjoy the garden, and rest easy in the knowledge that you're doing your bit for biodiversity.

Lughnasadh

Halfway between the summer solstice and the autumn equinox, at the beginning of August, comes the festival of Lughnasadh, which is also celebrated as Lammas, the time when we start to think about the harvest. One of the four Gaelic seasonal fire festivals along with Samhain, Imbolc, and Beltane, Lughnasadh's roots can be traced back to ancient Celtic tribes in Ireland, Scotland, Isle of Man, Wales, and other parts of the British Isles. It's a festival created to mark the harvest, to come together to offer thanks, to bake bread, and then sometimes to break some of this bread off and place it at field boundaries as an offering and to ward off evil. Most importantly, it is about gathering with others to celebrate the hard work of the year, the support of others, and the rewards of being a community.

We may have been planting our crops when the moon is new, waxing or full, watching them grow stronger as they draw on its energy, and harvesting, weeding, and composting as the moon wanes. I sometimes fall into these gardening patterns without giving any thought to the lunar phases. It's worth a thought before you dismiss it. But you're here, so I don't think you will, so give it a go. Work with the gravitational pull. It'll do no harm. Plant your annuals and fruits and vegetables that bear crops above ground between the day the moon is new to the day it is full—waxing. Plant perennials and root crops between the day after it is full to the day before it is new again—waning. The science behind what may seem like a myth bears up; as sap is drawn up or down trees according to light levels, so different plants benefit from gravity. It seems that gardeners have been doing this forever, or at least for as long as they've kept records about it, so who am I to judge? To the horror of scientists, I am very much of the mind that if it works, it works. Blind faith or a deep-down niggling feeling that this is how it should be—whichever way we want to describe our adherence to what might seem a bit of superstition is absolutely fine.

Opposite, left: Stepping stones lead through a clover-and-herb lawn to a bench of drystone walling in this family garden.

Opposite, middle: An old garden bench is enveloped in an array of cottage garden plants.

Opposite, right: A wildlife tower sits in the wildflower meadow, containing decorative elements as well as habitat-providing nooks.

Above: This garden was designed for a young couple needing a simple, inexpensive garden that could also provide ample wildlife habitat.

Right: A nest box for solitary bees is surrounded by nectar-rich plants.

When a Garden Looks Inwards

"Look to the location for your inspiration," they say, I say. But what happens when the genius loci, that spirit of the place that derives from way back when the Romans created their altars to the house spirits that watched over their homes, is simply not particularly thrilling?

In the middle of a modern city or town, there can be very little to grab on to in terms of a compelling sense of place. Of course we can think about what used to be where the garden is, what surrounds it now, and there will always be *something* interesting from the outside to work with, but as those Romans in their city villas also knew, sometimes the best thing to create privacy and sanctuary from the bustling, noisy *urbs* outside is to turn the garden's gaze inward, and make instead an atrium or courtyard haven, screening or even shutting out almost entirely what surrounds us. Sometimes it's worth celebrating that we can muster the will to create an atmosphere from scratch.

This garden in the heart of the city is overlooked by many neighbours. There's a beautiful plane tree in the next garden, a shelter for a very vocal robin whose bird's-eye view must otherwise be of interlocking rectangles and squares, urban enclosures delineated by Victorian terraces primly staking out everyone's territory. This is the deal you make for living in the city: people are simply going to see you going about your day. That's why so many city dwellers never even bother closing the curtains—if you want to look, feel free, but there's probably not much interesting going on in truth. But at the same time we need to feel as though we are in a nest of our very own. Gardens are

meant to feel safe and calm, to help distract us from the what-ifs and the whys of modern life and create a meditative state of mind. And if that sense of belonging, of our own roots down into the ground, isn't quite there at first, well, we can invent it.

The surrounding houses' brick façades create a staggered toytown view, where life goes on and movement passed through windows animates the scene. History is suggested by the layers of buildings' ages, whilst Tupperware skies remind us that we're in the middle of the city, with pea-souper smog days over but still in the memory as cars rumble by and buses with silent engines, intended to reassure, often unnerve as they try to glide by.

I want to escape from this. I want the same feeling that I experience when I'm inside my client's elegant home. Welcome. Warmth. Homeliness. Cosiness and elegance at the same time. There's a clear admiration for beauty: cranberry glass on shelves; on the walls are paintings of special places and dear ones.

Looking out from the kitchen where I sit with a cup of tea, the tree gives me a clue. I want this sense of seclusion. I want to be sheltered, up and over.

Inside a house, we have walls to denote use. Sometime in living areas, the walls are knocked down for ease of use, a space where the flow around is as important as the engagement of family. But sometimes, just sometimes, we do long for a tiny bit of get-away-from-it-all privacy. Outside, in this particular garden, this flow to the next space was the linchpin for what came next. The garden was to be enjoyed by a large family, creating a space for them

Opposite: A romantic, rose-filled garden feels particularly decadent when it's in the heart of a city.

Overleaf: Staggered beds leading down the garden create privacy and intrigue, since something new awaits

around every turn even in this relatively small space.

to get together; but that didn't mean that everyone needed to see each other all the time. And so it was that the space showed what it needed, animating and dividing itself up into four notional areas.

A terrace was the obvious follow-on from the house as you looked out of the kitchen window, and beyond that, a nook for this plantswoman to grow her roses, with a place for her to sit right in amongst the beds and borders. Two areas that can be seen as one, depending on how they're used. Viewed from the kitchen, it reads as one. Up close and personal on a bench, though, and you're in a rose garden in its own right.

The family's youngest child was already a teenager, so a place for play wasn't needed. No trampoline or climbing frames had to be shoehorned in. Yet outdoor play can be a stealthy starting point for encouraging the habit of seeing the outdoors as a friend, a place of respite and potential. Outdoor play—what does that become as we get older? Relaxation in the garden, time with friends, comfortable solitude, a change of scene, stimulation of the senses. So in a sense, an area for a more mature version of play was needed here. A place to sit either by oneself or to gather with others emerged in the form of two curved benches, immediately christened "banana benches" due to the curves necessary to fit two facing benches into this third of the garden's rooms, and the raised beds that emerged from behind the seating also provided more variation on planting bed spaces.

Left and above: A terrace just outside the kitchen provides a place to sit amongst ever-changing container displays.

147

Gatherings are always helped along by a drink or some food, and as the garden's owner is a brilliant hostess, her feeling was very much that a point of warmth in the form of a pizza oven would be just the thing to encourage her sons outside. She was right, and this fourth "room" was so created. We placed it at the back of this long garden in order to avoid it becoming a focal point, however. A bit like painting the floor of a room, in a garden with no external access you need to start building at the far end, and so it was that during a cold January and February, the builders could then make the most of the fire's heat.

Pergolas and uprights, simple in form and following the materials and the colours of the bifold kitchen doors, appear in the garden at points where they can frame or divide, or both, keeping terrace, flowers, seating, and cooking joined yet separate. The first of these is placed where the first flowerbeds end, creating a summer screen from the houses beyond, and as the climbing plants dangle down, it acts as another screen from the rest of the garden rooms. You potter through and come to the seating; staggered espaliered fruit trees in front of further metal uprights divide this seating from the cooking and eating area at the very end.

That's the "through" and the "above" dealt with; the immediate beyond, adjoining gardens, are deliberately forgotten by means of timber trellis to give the possibility of yet more planting, whilst still allowing through light on winter days. There's a touch of fun here—being great friends, the owner and her neighbour had previously chatted over the garden wall, and whilst they were both in agreement that there should be a visible division, they admitted that they'd be sad to lose these moments for easy chats. The solution to this came in the form of a 1970s-inspired hatch within the trellis, which could be flipped open to peek through.

And as for the roses everywhere, by pacing out rough dimensions and we worked out that we may be able to fit in around half a dozen roses at ground level. But that was just on the ground. It's good to remember that gardens are three-dimensional and therefore have volume—and that means a lot of planting opportunity. In this case, that meant maximising climbing roses. Against the walls and up the trellis, rambling roses would make their way up and over the pergolas and steel uprights. Whilst the walls could cope with more controlled climbers, we needed proper tumbling and drooping from any plants destined for pergolas. *Rosa* 'Adélaide d'Orléans' and *R.* 'Félicité-Perpétue' are two of my favourite performers for this gymnastic act: clusters of pale pink to white, the former elegantly relaxed in shape, the latter offers dainty pompoms perfect to pouffe through tangles of *Clematis* 'Etoile Violette', *Clematis alpina* 'Foxy', and *Clematis alpina* 'Willy'. Colour, as ever, is key. Pink reminds us of a place we once knew, either in reality or in a storybook, with happy-making shades tumbling though a garden full of charm.

You can just imagine the rose-lover in her kitchen, looking out upon this newly romanticised city plot, her view at night of blooms that seem to glow and flicker and catch the city light reflected off low clouds, glimmering gently. The sky is barely to be seen in a tangle of climbers and ramblers which have come together to provide flowery beams and colonnades across and along the whole of the garden.

Opposite: At the farthest end of the garden, *Rosa* Snow Goose (= 'Auspom') clothes one of the series of upright posts placed along the garden at intervals, to define individual usage areas.

Revelling in a River

Anyone who has visited the wonder that is Chatsworth House will know that the scale is extraordinary, the setting is out of this world, and the house is jaw-dropping. When I was invited to design an installation in this exciting location, I knew the scale had to be right. Whatever I did would in no way be able to compete with the glorious distractions around it; I would instead need to create a place which would sit and be part of the bigger place, a kind of a sculpture of a garden that could be looked through as much as looked into.

A house that has seen so much history, a house which is home to so much extraordinary beauty as well as the ghosts of so many, a warren of rooms upon rooms, each a treasure chest of eye-opening beauty. I once stayed there—and got so lost I actually had to call for help. I wished I'd left a trail of breadcrumbs back to where I was meant to be. "Do you need rescuing?" came a helpful voice down the end of the phone, in a reassuring tone that had clearly heard this plaintive request many times before.

Everything is beautifully large-scale here at Chatsworth, including the art amassed over centuries. The garden itself has been cultivated and designed and cherished for five hundred years, so being asked to create an installation anywhere near it was more than vaguely intimidating. Whatever I was going to do needed to make sense, have a fresh reason for existing.

While I was working, the sky was leaden grey and rumbling—those atmospheric conditions will forever remind me of the task at hand. An archaeologist with a brief was assigned to watch over me, to sign off on my every move. What do you do when you're in a

Simple steel rebar creates a sculpture that draws the eye in a garden designed to be looked through to the landscape beyond as much as looked into.

situation like this? I think a healthy dose of realistic thinking helps—knowing who you are (or aren't) and placing that against the majesty of what it is that you can see. Identifying that intention is key. I make green places, I take a look at the landscape around and absorb as much as I can of the spirit of the place in order to give what I'm creating some sense and semblance of unique being. In a location like this, you can't aspire to the greatness that is already there. I needed a gentle play, a bit of a romantic gesture, an experimental intervention designed to delight rather than wow. Landscape design is, here as always, really a question of choosing the correct scale.

On exploratory missions, there was much walking backwards and forwards and moving from spot to spot to choose a location for an installation. What kept appealing to me was the life force of the River Derwent. I wanted to use the riverbank, in my imagination still teeming with life from the tales of Ratty and Mole. Could I take over an enormous length of this riverbank without impacting it at all?

It turned out that, with some advice from ecologists and archaeologists, yes I could. I just wouldn't touch anything I didn't need to touch. I'd use materials that hadn't yet appeared here as art, avoiding the appearance of presuming to hope to match up in any

Opposite: A sketch for this installation shows how it weaves its meandering way down and along the river, in and out—an eddy of art that pools and flows as easily as the water itself.

Right, above and below: Steel rebar, though usually considered an industrial material, feels surprisingly appropriate to the natural setting when spaced in a rhythmic way amongst delicate plantings.

way to the richness elsewhere. Steel rebar, humble and modern, could have been a risky choice, but it managed somehow to look delicate as it one hundred metres of it wound its way in and out and down, cantilevered over the river, and anchored itself safely back against this extraordinary backdrop. Structural engineers had a heyday figuring out how it would support its own weight at the apex. As everything was lowered into place, I did ask myself why we'd gone just so big

and taken on something that could have been a lot smaller—but scale, though minuscule in comparison to the scale of other man-made elements here, was all. The sculpture was held by a mass of wildflowers interwoven with perennials, anchored by enormous scultptural, multi-stemmed field maples. Still but a dot on the landscape, the trees formed a link to the majestic parkland beyond.

Opposite, above and below: Huge, multi-stemmed field maples were chosen for inclusion here because of their size, as well as their sculptural trunks.

Above: Dahlias and salvias in bring the gentlest of structure into the wildflower meadow planting.

Overleaf: Any garden installed anywhere near Chatsworth House would in no way be able to compete per se with the glorious distractions around it. Instead I set out to create a garden space that enticed almost as

architectural follies do near other great houses—no one questions their presence, even while acknowledging they're not the main attraction, and they always feel special and as though they belong.

Embracing History

This London garden, now a haven for wildlife, took into account many different intents during its inception. Making a place for the family, of course, but a place for all the nonhumans too. Layers of green, shelter, food, and habitat in place of a lawn. And plenty of roses in borders, of course. Previously there was nothing, simply a nondescript space hugged by beautiful trees. Long conversations helped the clients achieve a characterful feel of romance, a place for all the family, and a garden that works with the enormous plane trees both in and around its location within in a conservation area. As the house's beautiful Georgian walls were restored and clothed in leaves, details and clues of how the house and garden had once been used were picked out and pieced together to tell a new story that helped to bring the garden back to full life.

Today, a vegetable garden with beds and espaliered fruit trees sits to one side, enclosed by historic boundary walls. Native plants grow happily amid ornamental perennials, and generous shrubs including hydrangeas, dogwoods, and sambuca (for structure) grow under trees such as amelanchier, magnolia, cercis, and acer for a continuous display of blossom and leaf colour. An oak pergola smothered with climbing roses and clematis leads to a separate wing of the house, a guest cottage, creating privacy and a sense of arrival at the same time. A reclaimed York stone terrace leads to a covered outdoor kitchen tucked away to one side, out of view. A true family garden, it is a space for children's play, for entertaining friends and family, and for two very happy cats.

If you know your house has been around for a while, a bit of research can go a long way toward giving you ideas of how to move it successfully into the future. A delve into the archives can reveal much. When I first visited these clients, their wish list included an orchard, fish pond, vegetable garden, and an octagonal summerhouse. These were very specific requests, so, duly noted, I went about doing some research just to see what had been there before that we might restore or build up again. Visibly Georgian, this house actually turned out to have Tudor roots; it had replaced a building dating from the fourteenth century. For seven hundred years, people had lived here, produced food here. It also turned out that, uncannily, there had originally been an orchard, fish pond, vegetable garden, and . . . an octagonal summerhouse.

All these elements had long, long since disappeared. No one, when we were initially discussing the garden, knew that these elements had previously existed, and yet the current owners clearly had somehow absorbed the sense of these ideas. The garden had told them what it wanted back. I found myself here looking at a spot that had very much been in the countryside, which now, although in the middle of the expanded city, still retains a sense of that former life.

As this house's Georgian walls were gradually restored, details about the history of the site were picked out, pieced together, and translated to help the garden tell a new story and to bring it back to life.

Opposite and above: A new pond was created at the end of the garden, with a stepping-stone route past a gentle waterfall. The leaves of *Acer palmatum* 'Atropurpureum' reflect the reddish tone of the brick and tiles of the historic walls and buildings so very well; in spring, the tulip palette does the same.

Websites and magazines might have us believe that glamorous gardens necessarily involve large lawns edged by formal plantings along strictly horizontal and vertical axes. Size, however, doesn't dictate any of this. A large house, grand in appearance, is often given a garden that's austere and ostentatious, with sharp lines cut into it by hard materials and vast bodies of topiary quickly chosen as a group for their impressive size with little consideration to what carefully considered individual forms could instead give to the garden. This is predictable, and can be so draining to the overall atmosphere one actually expects from such a property. I mourn this poverty of spirit. When this happens, it means that no one has really taken the luxury of time to consider, properly consider, the house, the place, or their joint history. Maybe I'm mistaken, and these gardens are indeed made just to look at, to admire, to create awe, like the fifty manicured hectares of Emperor Nero's Domus Aurea in Rome, a place built as an outward symbol of a man's importance, wealth, and power. In this London garden, however, the absolute opposite was the case. This was now a place for a family.

This city garden had a straight-edged terrace, pergola, and outdoor kitchen—that was all the geometry needed. If you've really got under its skin, a place usually offers up its meaning and helps us create a sense of what it wants to be. Here in London, the city itself already full enough of hard lines and surfaces, curving lines now bend the borders in and out,

sweeping around trees to create expansive as well as cosier places. The lawn feels safe as a place to play, a place to encourage the children out into the garden and down to the vegetable plot, where Tudor-inspired brick paths crisscross productive beds.

A small pond found a hollow of a home near where its enormous predecessor had once lain; stepping stones, for fun rather than necessity, lead over the water to that octagonal summerhouse, a retreat in the green in all the layers of green that hide as well as entice. There's a shed in the far corner, and the space behind the garden shed is planted as prettily as the area in front. We often think of the "far end" behind a shed or as the deepest, darkest corner not worthy of attention, but, especially in a town garden, every square centimetre of space is precious, so it seems a shame to ignore any plot, even if the compost heap/bins/air conditioning vent have been squeezed in there out of sight, out of mind. In this garden, it was the ideal spot in which to secret away the utilities, but just because it was a utilitarian area didn't mean that the spot should be relegated to a future of dark nothingness. So, with the intention of giving it an air of cultivated chaos, its unassuming service path was framed with ferns, hydrangeas, and grasses all happy in the shady, damp area. This mini-glade of hydrangeas has surpassed itself as far as late summer interest is concerned, and the client has now put a bench there to ensure that they get a chance to sit and enjoy every corner the garden has to offer.

Right: Grasses and foliage provide ample texture here; their height and form enhance the feeling of deep privacy that the wall beyond enforces.

Overleaf: *Rosa x odorata* 'Mutabilis' and *Hydrangea arborescens* 'Annabelle' provide hints of gentle colour as we look from the pond through to the garden beyond.

Always on Display

With the pleasure of shore-front living comes the tradeoff of knowing a property must by nature be completely exposed—to the sea, salt, winds, beachcombers. Any idea of privacy is banished but the view is worth it; indeed, the whole point of this garden was that it must settle in, complement but ultimately cede to an even grander vista.

Gardens by the sea of course have to perform in site conditions that visitors usually consider scenic but plants tend to consider harsh. The true strength of any hard material that's optimistically labelled "marine grade" is sure to be tested to its very limit in a place where there's truly no shelter, no leeward side in sight. There's no point in fighting over niggling negatives when a garden is in this situation, but to use them as a creativity-inducing stricture to find how to turn all elements into positives.

This building site had been chosen for a new house precisely because of its enviable position. When I first visited and enquired about the direction of the prevailing wind, everyone present fell about laughing at the ridiculousness of the question—the wind comes from *everywhere*. It carries the salty spray, and the nearer the water comes as the tides push in, the greater nature's impact. And all this on a twice-daily cycle. High and low, changing the view, changing everything. With this literal ebb and flow and, vying for attention, a horizon as big as you like, it became clear that whatever plants were to go in front would require a sharp solidity to remain relevant as everything else around them continued to shift in colour and form. The sea retreats, becoming sfumatoed and

Since the horizon and the sea will always be focal points for this property, the garden was designed to be a foreground to that great vista, to sit in harmony with the elements rather than fighting against them.

smudged into the sky, and then comes back into roaring focus, sharpening the non-outlines of all.

Hence the clear white rendered walls, a bolder element than might appear in other gardens. Whilst in a suburban garden a dazzling white can puzzle us against bleak fence panels and grey skies, here by the beach, the white creates light-reflecting and light-scattering wavelengths of sunlight. There's an obvious link to the materials of the house as well, but there's more: If it's a cloudy day, those clouds are going to take up half the picture, and if the sky is totally blue, the white walls beneath will form a good contrast with the wide band of blue above. In addition, the backdrop helps manipulate colour and form to work with the foreground: the standout white is applied to a shape that doesn't stand out against the house and instead appears something of a continuation of architectural intent.

An elliptical wall provides the practical elements of seating, along with a touch of privacy, and the windbreak that human use of this garden demands. The first step in arriving at this shape was to identify the corner best for seating; the sharpness of both the shape and colour telescope the viewer's attention to this corner. This was the intention, but at the same time there's the intrigue in not being forced to see the entire area at once. Direction and journey, then, created by winding decked paths making their way over the sand, stop that mad dash of our focus to the oblique white shape which, when seen from a foreshortened angle, gives a sense of being round, enclosing, inviting.

Even if you think you're not going to have time to make use of it, a place here and there to sit is calm-inducing in a garden. It reminds us subliminally that taking a break is an option. So I plan these spots in.

Above: Carved oak posts and maritime rope create the simplest of boundaries, fittingly distinguishing the end of the beach from the edge of the garden without interrupting the view. Opposite: Man-made dunes create the contours which give privacy to the entertaining area.

Beauty in simplicity; small but considered details such as having a house's name carved into an oak post can often be omitted from a final garden due to budget constraints. This client supported these enhancements, which together create a garden full of unexpected moments of wonder.

And if you don't use it, trust me, your friends will. Once they're there, they always, inevitably, get used. This house's entertaining spaces move from inside out, and one wants to feel that there are options depending on the weather, but at the same time this area has to beckon people out.

Gusts are as much a part of the moving soul of this garden as plants or hardscape, but they are frankly also a bit of a deterrent when it comes to the idea of relaxing outside. Most importantly, this seat has to be designed in conjunction with its function, which, in this garden, is to celebrate whatever conditions nature blows in. Common-sense solutions are always appealing, and so it was that the idea came about of creating a natural fortification, developed through detailed study of the neighbouring dunes. Walking through these grass-knitted hills of sand which close in and open up, creating a landscape of changing levels as you make your way through them—they're magical. The absolute magic of this place wasn't to be shut out of the garden. It was part of the landscape. It had to be let in.

So it was that the garden's dunes came to be. The sand was pushed and suggested into low mounds, which biodegradable matting then held in place until the native marram grass could take on the seemingly impossible role of knitting together innumerable individual grains of sand. The seating area, the entertaining space with its welcoming curves, would be tucked into this, visible from the house but invisible from the beach. Curves wind through the garden, taking a cue from the undulating mountains of sand beyond.

We sawed into the matting on windy days, making pockets for the planned plants and knowing full well they would soon by joined by other volunteers: *Eryngium maritimum, Crambe maritima, Armeria maritima.* Those tough plants didn't need our help—the garden's existence was invitation enough to this bunch of seaside-dwellers. The clue is in the name. Poppies, their red expressive, spontaneous brushstrokes

capturing the vibrancy and movement of nature, easily joined in with the gatecrashers, putting up an impressive canvas against the marram grass that has always called this windy ridge with a view home.

Armeria maritima and *Silene uniflora*, above, have been joined by a poppy that happily self-seeded here, below.

Two Dreams in One Design

The garden is a place to fulfil your dreams of having a garden for garden's sake and also a place to fulfil your dreams of how you live life outdoors. Whilst sometimes everyone's ideas are fully aligned, the chances are that the more people who will be using that garden, the more ideas, ideals, hopes, imaginary pictures, dislikes, and loves will be involved.

When I first went to visit this great big hole in the ground, which was all that remained after a basement had been built, it became clear that my job would be to bring together the dreams of two people who admitted that each person's hopes for the garden stood at the furthest pole from the other's. It was the garden of a plant lover and a sports lover; to fulfil both their dreams, I would have to tease out from the emptiness a place where there could be both a retreat scented by an envelope of roses, a place of calm and creativity… and a place to play football. Desires are valid, whatever the subject: both had a right to exist. The designer's role is figuring out the magic that will enable as many aspirations as possible to fold into one another and emerge as place that makes everyone happy.

Some people find a wish list useful when it comes to creating a garden; they're a good starting point, but these can easily become a simply a tick list of various parts that, if all are included, can actually obscure the purpose or clarity of a garden's overarching design. A shopping list approach can lead to a spot that feels like it's missing soul, turning design into a perfunctory process. The performative can drain the mission of life. Stepping back helps sprinkle the elements that make magic, a whole. Step away from the enticing glamour of a shiny idea you've seen in a magazine and go back to what your garden is all about: you.

Drystone walls and terraces separate the part of this family garden meant for general recreation from a sport court concealed behind.

This garden is for a large family who will continue to want different things from this space as both they and the garden grow. Play is key here. A sense of fun, of the exhilaration from running around and the joy of joining in games even if by the simple of act of sitting down and cheering from the sidelines. All tied up in the love of plants that had been expressed at the very beginning of the conversation.

I've been asked to include many different types of play areas in gardens. Sometimes, it can be as simple as incorporating a swing, or room to run around and play, to play hide-and-seek with areas for enclosure and surprise. It's simplest to begin by sketching out how imaginary routes around the garden might suggest themselves as I try to accommodate various uses. In a strongly rectilinear space such as this, curving paths can always be helpful to soften, divert, beckon, and provide surprise around an unexpected turn.

Invisible from the area of the garden closest to the house, a small amphitheatre on the garden's uppermost level creates a private space for people to gather and to watch the action on the pitch.

Above: Curves soften hard stone walls while planting deftly obscures what lies beyond the steps.

Right, above and below: A series of gently winding pathways and steps are designed to slow the journey through the garden, creating interest and intrigue until the visitor reaches the sports area at the far end of this city space.

It quickly became clear that flowers and fun, the two main features in this garden, could actually be divided up quite simply in this long, rectangular city garden—nearly in half, in fact. A lower-level lawn adjacent to the kitchen, surrounded by terraced beds filled with flowering shrubs and perennials, could create an area for lounging about in while the terracing would create the most pleasant type of visual partition: a foliage-filled and flowery one. Scribbles on paper turned themselves into routes circling other beds as they work their way up to the next level; their destination is a very clear stone amphitheatre, its curves (form) distracting attention from the neighbouring gardens (function) and focusing us in on the game (purpose).

For there is a place to play up on the second level. It isn't immediately obvious; look closely and you'll spy a hint of where the terraces lead; netting surrounds a green area big enough for children's five-a-side football, a smooth wall for practising tennis shots against. You can't see it all unless you're up there, but once you are, you feel far from the house, from the city, and you can focus on being outdoors and just having fun. What it's all about. These spaces are future-proofed in their use; a place for younger members to watch a match, the stone seating is equally popular with older members of the family as they hang out with friends.

Layers—both vertical and horizontal—mean this garden can't be seen all at once. Winding routes and changing elevations provided by full and varied plantings, drystone walls, and curving paths work together to conceal a playful secret in part of this garden buzzing with pollinators.

Above, left and right: Shrubs including roses, hydrangeas, and pittosporum provide the plant mass and volume that the hard landscaping needs in order to soften it.

Right: *Cirsium rivulare* 'Atropupureum' complements the tone of the existing brick boundary walls well.

Making a Show Garden

To be successful, a show garden needs to have a client of its own, complete with strong personality and sense of self—never mind that they're imaginary or that the garden is temporary. Part of the pleasure in creating a show garden is for the designer to allow these figment-of-one's-imagination clients to take various forms while mulling the possibilities—One person? No, two. A couple, who grows again—a family—and off into fantciful worlds the mind goes, fully justified in its wanderings as it digs around for a reason for the garden to exist. The reason has to be substantive. Beauty alone can't be an excuse for a show garden; this never works, as I've learned from an experiment of my own where I allowed a heavy message to prevail over personality. When a visitor looks at any show garden, they should feel scooped up and transported. If not, the mind starts to niggle and question, and quickly identifies that garden as simply an unreal and unsatisfying space.

Atmosphere will always win the day, and note here that I'm not talking about winning show medals. Inasmuch as atmosphere is a deeply subjective, just as in colour where one person's lavender is another person's lilac, when I see a visitor who is voicing an absolutely adamant opinion that the garden in front of them should have been awarded gold, even that it should have been awarded best in show, I can truthfully say to any crestfallen designer clutching a medal that might not be the hue they'd hoped, "There's your gold medal!" If you have taken a person to whom the garden is completely new along with you on your mission to create a memorable place, a feeling, out of absolutely nothing at all, then you've won.

A show garden is all about creating an experience for onlookers, and that should be transmitted whether they are viewing it in person as a visitor to a flower show, watching it on a screen from far-flung places, or even leafing through a magazine or a book featuring it years later. If a space is only to exist for a week (unless, of course it's hopefully repurposed elsewhere afterwards in some form), you have to compel people instantly with its story. A design that tries only to address imaginary medal-winning goals will just never do. It has to be imbued with a sense of meaning, a touch of romance. It has to have *soul*.

Although these gardens have a legacy, and are rebuilt in a future home, there often isn't any sense of time, of the past. Even the boundaries aren't real. So how does one go about walking them, beating them and getting to know them, to give the sense that a garden exists in a place with a sense of place? There's adversity in all of this, and I can tell you honestly that every time I begin the physical process of building one of these gardens, I ask myself what madness, what impulse led me to think that I could create something out of literally nothing. This never occurs when I'm making actual gardens in actual places, because they offer *some* starting point: geography, ecology, personalities, *something*. But when I first set foot on the showground, I wonder what on earth possessed me to try out a hitherto-untested idea in front of an audience of hundreds of thousands. Up for scrutiny. Up for judgement. Up for debate and criticism. Up for show.

This feeling, which is more a sense of the surreal rather than fear or any form of imposter syndrome, comes and goes as you create the garden. It crashes

Doris, the name we gave to the sweetest little caravan you ever did see, peeks out from behind *Viburnum plicatum* f. *tomentosum* 'Mariesii'.

Left, above and below: In any garden, well-conceived extra details are the final touches that truly create atmosphere; in a show garden, as here, clues about the imaginary inhabitants of the garden are vital to injecting a sense of life.

Opposite: Dainty pastel flowers keep the mood feminine and cheerful, including *Chaerophyllum hirsutum* 'Roseum', top, *Rosa* 'Our Beth', left below, and *Geranium pratense* 'Mrs. Kendall Clark', right below.

down on you when the rain starts falling and just doesn't stop, halting construction and delaying an impossibly tight timetable. When the sun comes out and vitamin D starts tickling the crew again, spirits soar: the leaves start to burst out of those tightly curled buds on a forlorn-looking tree by which you've set so much store, so the show will go on, all will be well. Then you come across a vast piece of concrete, identifiable as a leftover from a garden on the same site ten years previous, which was clearly so tricky to move that the builders of that space had clearly decided, rather naughtily, to abandon it there. It only takes a discovery such as this, which has very bad implications for what you'd been planning (for a year) to build on that exact spot, to pause the

proceedings once more. And then there's a delay... and then back on the wheel of doubt and optimism we go again.

So this caravan caused a bit of a stir when she trundled onto the RHS Chelsea Flower Show building site early one May. Mud-covered landscape contractors stopped in their tracks as they came up to investigate something that turned out to inspire nostalgia in many: memories of caravanning. She was a 1950s Fisher Holivan, and her name was Doris. On the one and only camping trip I've ever undertaken, staying in a very cool Airstream on the Isle of Wight, I had noticed the sweetest little vintage caravan in the far corner of the field. Full of personality and clues to character,

Above: A sculpted oak bench with a minimalist form is beautiful to look at and surprisingly comfortable to lounge on.

Opposite, left: A hammock, essential to any good caravan excursion, provides another secret spot to relax.

Opposite, right: When we designed a garden for the whole family, we included four-legged friends.

she intrigued me; I made a mental note that one day we would meet again. Fast-forward a couple of years and my promise to myself was realised as I tracked her down and she made it all the way to centre of London, the inspiration for a show garden designed for a family.

We placed her, fully decorated on the inside, down a path at the back of the garden, a focal point behind a grid of straight lines crisscrossing the space. These simple lines supported plantings in layers and created routes and journeys round to a range of seating opportunities, some in quieter spots, some less so. There was a truly traditional feel to the planting but, with a bit of a shake-up too. We had roses and perennials in good old pinks, blues, whites, and violets, but also a wine cooler doubling

as a quilted-aluminium rill. A bench floats above this water, and a hammock idles behind a screen.

For me, no family is complete without a four-footed friend. And so how could I design a family garden for the RHS Chelsea Flower Show without including a space for a dog? The resulting kennel was inspired by the shape of the caravan, even with a matching porthole window. I wanted it to have more than one function, though, and so the idea of the herby roof garden was born. Tiny alpine straw-berries and thyme made for a fragranced topper for this dog's delight. Thinking practically, this tiny roof garden needed to drain, and so runoff was directed into a downpipe which fed into a water bowl. All vet-approved, of course.

Venetian Colour

Inspiration can come from places as varied as a single plant to a long overseas voyage to a detail from history still lurking around a property's foundation, so explaining how I get the ideas for gardens often can sound either vague or scattered as I pull bits from here, bobs from there and attempt to weave them into a whole. Sometimes, though, there's one definite spark, a lightbulb moment. Here, the simple act of gazing at a view brought about exactly one of those moments.

A few years ago, I'd been walking alongside a canal in Venice, where this "alongside" is known as a *fondamenta*, a pavement which both enables pedestrians and also does the extra job of helping to hold up the houses up. It was a place set back away from the crowds, and I'd been gazing and marvelling, as is the way in this city, at the light, the colours, moments of stillness amongst the bustle. Everyone was busily not occupying themselves: *dolce far niente*. Life in public on full, unapologetic display.

When there's a surface of water within a view, light bounces everywhere, making colours seem doubly vibrant. Taking a moment to stop and make my brain wrap itself around what was going on, I worked out that the combination of colours the Venetian houses had been painted had been chosen to take advantage of this effect. Shades of pink and peach and yellow and orange that conjure up all those food-related similes that we've come to associate with a palette that perhaps isn't usual, but which absolutely works here, set off by the green-blue of the water at their base. A list of colour no-nos gathered over a lifetime

Arches that recall Venetian loggias are a central feature in this contemporary show garden, placed here as a series of pavilions that stand over pools and rills that are meant to recall the city's famous canals.

came to mind: blue and green should never be seen, brown only in town, pink and yellow do not go. It's usually at a moment exactly like that, when I become conscious that for one reason or another I *shouldn't* do something, that I decide to give it a go.

And so it was that I brought those colours back to England, showing them together in front of a great-big public audience at the RHS Chelsea Flower Show in 2019. Wedgwood was sponsoring, and they supported the longing I had to show something completely new, to celebrate the impact that colour can have, and to give people fresh ideas as well as challenge existing ideas of what can and can't be planted together, what makes a successful colour scheme. Indeed, Wedgwood colours from various collections

also served as inspiration. I created the garden and held my breath, wondering if I'd gone just a bit too far. Would people enjoy it? Talk about it in the positive? The combination of sherbet colours of pinks, lemons, and corals marked this garden out as something different. I'd seen the colours in action back in Venice, and although I knew that the London light would be very, very different, it seemed to me that this whole no-yellow-with-pink thing was a bit of a dead-end statement, and that as long as you pinpoint the right shade, anything can go with anything.

The Wedgwood Garden references Etruria, the home and Staffordshire village that Josiah Wedgwood built for workers 260 years ago. The space reflects the entrepreneurial and innovative

Above, left to right: *Rosa* 'Buff Beauty', *R.* 'Bonica', and *Iris* 'Pink Charm' bring the colours of Venetian buildings to Chelsea.

Opposite: Challenging existing ideas of what can and can't be planted together, this garden was an experiment in new ideas for planting colour schemes; pinks, peaches, and oranges harmonise with the stone and steel of the garden's structures.

At Iford Manor, which proved a second and closer-to-home source of inspiration for the Chelsea Flower Show garden, details drawn from antiquity meld seamlessly with the Wiltshire landscape.

spirit of the Wedgwood founder by combining classical motifs and designs in a contemporary form. Water unifies the garden and moves throughout the space with purpose, connecting key elements and echoing the canals and watercourses of the past that were fundamental to Wedgwood's production line and industry.

The arch was a fundamental shape in this garden: familiar and ever-present, humble enough to be used in workers' accommodations yet also immediately calling to mind elaborate Italian loggias, travel, history. Whatever the reasoning, all agree that arches are very satisfying to look at and so they became a central feature in this contemporary space, itself inspired by classical architecture. A series of pavilions and arches nestled amongst waterways and art has been interpreted and reinterpreted successfully for centuries.

The inspiration for these shadows and frames and screens of structure come from a place much nearer to home, one of the most beautiful places in England. In the most magical of Wiltshire valleys, nestled into a dip, the honeystone façade of Iford Manor rises serenely and steadily out of the contours of the land, instantly warming and welcoming everyone who approaches. When we think about those who have gone before, they still tread here at Iford. The garden can't be fully seen or grasped except by travelling through it; it reveals itself as it leads you up, then left, then right, and up again.

Anything could happen, you feel, as you wander around, catching glimpses of someone, something itchingly familiar as you go. Or was it simply a shadow, Aslan the cat as he makes his way slowly and knowingly along? Iford is a garden of mysteries and mellow magic, a continuing source of inspiration, a guaranteed peaceful day out. And most importantly, it continues to grow into the twenty-first century. It's a masterclass in framing and scale and context and layout: Harold Peto certainly knew what he was doing. If we followed certain strict approaches to design, it would have to follow that the columns from other times and other places he incorporated at Iford shouldn't work against the quintessentially English landscape. But they do. Antiquity melds seamlessly with locality—with a little help from some well-chosen plants.

Iford Manor was the place foremost in my mind when I was designing the Wedgwood garden we see here. It reminded me that a focal point needn't be seen dead centre, nor does it need to be entirely contained within a frame; it can start there, of course, but then continue and travel and flow. Peto managed the view and led the eye up over and away into the landscape so very, very brilliantly, using architectural elements from another land with wonderful results. Although from a different time and a different culture, they work. Borrowed landscape at its most literal and best.

A City Jewel

In a little tucked-away corner of London sits a garden jewel. No one but its owners know it's there, it's a kind of garden Narnia as you enter the house from a busy street, pass through, and step out of the kitchen door. As you do so, all thoughts of the city disappear, as the plants scoop you up and take you on a romantic journey through roses and herbaceous planting which is as soft as it is wild.

The charm of this cottage has its roots in the architecture, unusual in an urban environment and seductive as the internal layout leads you from room to room. There are twists and turns, higgles and piggles, and I felt that the planting outside should create this same atmosphere. Ups and downs were needed, routes obscured and then opening up and revealing new elements as if by magic. The previously manicured garden would need give way to something with character that would truly anchor the place to *its* place.

Height is just one of the ways of creating this rhythm and movement in a garden. Pergolas and arbours, maligned by some, are I think some of the very best ways to create changes of level, and thereby creating interest as new focal points are created. A pergola very much has to serve a purpose—whether it's dividing a space or suggesting a route to somewhere, it needs to be of use in order to sit well in its location. Its structure should take its beginnings from something nearby, too, whether it's from the house or something that's visible beyond, something needs to link the new to the existing.

I see these structures as opportunities for new plants. Nothing makes me sadder than a series of naked arches placed along a garden, placed there for the sake of design rather than being seen as an opportunity to introduce more climbers and ramblers.

In this garden, the structures really do live up to their intended purpose. From the earliest white and primrose yellow Banksian roses, through midsummer to autumn and the last of the repeat-flowering English rambling roses, wherever you look, there are flowers at nose level, eye level, and overhead. Clematis are planted to bloom before and after the roses—sometimes they stick to their intended timings, and sometimes they surprise us; each year, the anticipation of what they're going to do keeps us guessing and engaged.

All this height requires balance, the loosest kind of balance in a garden, which I want to feel as relaxed as possible. As ever, there's more planting than hardscape in this space, with small paths picking their way through flowerbeds as the garden extends along the house's length. These beds create multiple opportunities: for planting, of course, but what they also do is link the different areas as you travel through them, creating atmospheres which are the same but different as you wander through the garden.

The planting design of these beds was key to the atmosphere of this place. Manicured formality wouldn't create the desperately needed anchor to the house, and low planting would leave a feeling of insufficiency. Again, height was needed: tall plants would balance the pergolas, but at the same time, there are views through the garden that I don't want to block.

A range of Benton irises stand elegantly in a city garden also teeming with rambling and shrub roses.

This is where those naked stems come in again. *Valeriana officinalis* and *V. pyrenaica*, with their small, rounded domes of flowers held above sturdy stems are a solid enough way of creating a planted transparent screen, whilst at the same time catching the light and becoming temporary focal points as they make their way through the garden. Growing up through a foliage foundation layer providing by the surrounding herbaceous perennials, their hint of unruliness, combined with the irises, conjures up that atmosphere of romance that I'm after.

This garden is as much about the irises as it is about the roses.

What is it about the iris, this plant of beauty, elegance, associated in Greek myth with Iris, goddess of the rainbow, a plant beloved of Van Gogh, that is so very seductive? It's a plant which so easily anthropomorphises into a graceful lady, serene and majestic. And for a warm place, with the luxury of space, irises create a show of colour that takes up the flag from the tulips, which often, but not always, have disappeared by the time of the arrival of highly unique standards, falls, signals, petals, and often beards.

It's a plant that works well in the heat, but it isn't a lover of the wet, and so care has to be taken when we plant them.

Above: *Digitalis purpurea* and *Valeriana officinalis* add vertical geometry and particular pops of colour.

Opposite: A sundial by early-twentieth-century artist Archibald Knox, known for his work with Liberty in its heyday, is an intriguing focal point amongst the scented roses and perennials.

Some of the many irises in this garden include, clockwise from top left: *Iris* 'Benton Caramel', *I.* 'Benton Olive', *I.* 'Benton Menace', *Iris sibirica* 'Perry's Blue', and *I.* 'Benton Duff'.

In a garden where I can't have that dedicated iris bed so often seen in France and Italy, where the flowers arrive earlier, in April, I instead sweep and dot them through a border. Their presence is fleeting, and in my own garden I'm out every morning detaching the withered flowers as they make their way up the stems. Earlier than the summer heat, their blooming isn't affected by later water shortages; in fact they love to bathe their knobbly rhizomes in the sun.

As I wandered around on my first visit, there was something about this house's architectural details and existing ornamental items that turned my thoughts immediately to the intoxicating shades of the Benton irises, bred by Cedric Morris in the

1940s. If you've never seen a Benton iris in real life, I urge you to avail yourself of a few of them if you possibly can. They stand proudly and gracefully, elegant in their delicacy.

Yet even further beyond the beauty of their form is the sheer exquisiteness of their colourings and marking. Murky shades blend together to create mysterious colours for which you can't think of a name, but which really need a name—trying to invent them is a pleasant pastime while we wander the garden.

Walkways and pergolas clothed in climbing and rambling roses divide this riverside garden into a series of unique rooms.

Left: *Rosa* Queen of Sweden (= 'Austiger') and *Centranthus ruber* 'Albus' combine with textures that act as a foil to the other.

Opposite: The intense royal purple of *Geranium phaeum* 'Lily Lovell'.

A Penthouse Garden

Wherever you are, never forget to look up. We're so busy looking where we walk, choosing our path, avoiding the literal and metaphorical trips that can change a day from good to bad in a split second. So focused are we on the ground plan, the way ahead on the horizontal plane, that we sometimes forget what's all around us. The branches of shade trees. Clouds. The possibility offered by vertical space. Volume. Infinite cubic metres of possibility. And a different point of view.

Perched above a busy London square, this glimpse of green exists improbably far up and away from where the plants might have thought their roots would ever reach. To plan this city rooftop, I also found that I needed to look up for inspiration, break out of my own ground-based habits. But even more than that, I needed to look *beyond*. There's something about a roof terrace that fights a little with logic: a garden in the sky? There's a different landscape, a different sense of place to create. Here, historic spires and newer buildings became both focal points and veils, hinting at ways we could stop the eye and create different layers of interest to look through and gaze upon. The hard verticals soften with distance, gently pulling further and further away. Rooftop views framed by plants mellow the effect of man-made imposition, allowing us to marvel at architecture instead of just feel hemmed in by concrete and stone. The urban setting here gave me many clues as to how to move forward with kneading a wish list into this malleable lump of potential. A place to cool off, a place to relax, a place to be with friends, a place that feels soft underfoot, a place for pollinators. A place to enjoy the sun, and to feel sheltered from it. A place to be private. A place to enjoy the view.

Notions that at first seem to clatter into each other, instead need to be separated out and their possibilities explored. Sun and shade were easy—include a large umbrella that can be folded down when not in use to avoid the windy day dilemma. But a place that is both screened and open—how could that work? Let's imagine the terrace being used on a sunny day. A splash in the pool, someone bathing in the sun, a guest excitedly noticing the spire of a church designed by Sir Christopher Wren. It's as this picture builds up that the requirements of the place start to dictate themselves. What could enhance and not restrict all these activities simultaneously? Plants as architecture start the process, and so lightweight, rooftop-tolerant birches in pots ample enough for their roots, are used to draw the eye even farther upwards and make the most of all those metres of vertical volume that are ours to play with. Their upright forms create interest here, and also privacy, and even more importantly, they frame views.

These multi-stemmed silver birch splay up in an inverted cone of a framework, counteracted by sentries of fiercely upright *Calamagrostis* x *acutiflora* 'Karl Foerster', a grass flexible enough for windy rooftop conditions, but that never ever gives in. The ever-important mounds of geranium and alchemilla are soft against the slightly-sturdier domes of pittosporum, while blurring comes from gaura, which remains steady and productive for what seems like a very long time, and then surprises us by going on

On this city rooftop, plants were chosen in tones that would look well against the ever-changing skies.

even longer than that. Other plants make this place attractive to users who aren't human as well; beech hedges, grass in living soil, wildflowers at the perimeter all offer amenity to wildlife that is accustomed to cruising on the breeze at a height of seven storeys.

As well as doing the jobs described, these plants all allow for appreciation—sometimes nearly forgotten in a city—as to how the wheel of the year turns. As summer comes and the plants emerge, so our trips out into the garden to see what's going on become more frequent. A celebration over a bloom here, some more serious pruning there, and a continued study of how the native flowers perform each year. It gives the chance to come back to something familiar and to carry out our work, which makes us feel good. Room for spontaneity as well as ritual.

The impressionists caused a scandal by embracing the colour violet, by promoting it as the colour of air—whether imagined, or correct, or simply smog as some now think, I think they were on to something, as it's certainly a colour that felt appropriate here. Lilacs and violets, bluish pinks and pinkish blues suggested themselves as hues and tones that would arrange themselves gracefully against the sky.

The positive psychological effects of blue are associated with inducing calm and serenity. It is said to help reduce mental stress, with dark blue in particular creating an atmosphere conducive to focus and concentration. Light blue creates a sense of space, it reminds us of trips to the sea and sitting by lakes; from there our minds easily wander to travel, water, and sky. Pink communicates compassion, innocence.

In art, the use of pink traditionally symbolized youth and romance, not sickly-sweet defenceless femininity as happens today. Think of the peachy pastel pink of the woman's dress in Jean-Honoré Fragonard's rather raunchy *The Swing*—as sugary as you can get, but it's pure Rococo eroticism.

There's a sense of airiness, freedom, lightheartedness up here. You feel properly away from it all as the layers of planting and hedges screen and lead you round. A rooftop garden is a luxury in itself, so perhaps it is that the simplicity of the palette is the "fault" of sky beyond. This garden is a new green space, carved out of thin violet air.

Opposite, left: A small rooftop plunge pool has a backdrop of beech hedging for privacy.

Opposite, right: *Calamagrostis* x *acutiflora* 'Karl Foerster' provides a visual border for the garden without blocking the view. Real grass feels is a welcome and soft addition to the roof.

Above: The sprightly stems of *Oenothera lindheimeri* wave gently in the rooftop breezes.

Overleaf: Rooftop views framed by plants help us to marvel at the surrounding architecture instead of feeling hemmed in by concrete and stone.

Placemaking for Leisure

It's hard to believe that there was nothing here when I first visited—not a tree, not a shrub, not a single perennial. Just a big open space. Normally, the landscape surrounding any space is everything—it gives you clues about interventions even when you just want to screen it out. But when you're faced with a completely blank canvas, it's critical to decide on a proposed atmosphere for the final place before you impose anything on the land, to embrace what is going to be without necessarily knowing exactly how that "going to be" will manifest.

Here, a spa's swimming pool building went up, and the garden grew around it. Think clay and bare and open, with some distant trees scattered across parkland and falling into the romance of the Wealden landscape beyond. If you continue along this land-scape for a few miles, you'll see the same backdrop, but viewed through the magnificent opening of the barn at Sissinghurst, the garden that encapsulates romance, history, optimism, plantsmanship, and epitomises the creation of a beautiful garden for garden's sake.

In lieu of an Elizabethan tower to serve as a clue of inspiration, however, I had only a modern building housing an indoor swimming pool as my defining element, with a tennis court next door. That was it. This, a place for leisure, a place where I could straight away imagine chatterings of fun, murmuring of voices whiling away a Sunday afternoon over a glass of something cold. This is what defined the place for me—envisioning the comings and goings of those who would come here for relaxation. These were my characters for the stage set that had to be created here.

In this garden full of white blooms, *Hydrangea arbo-rescens* 'Annabelle' provides a mass of striking yet simple colour against the box-pleached hornbeams.

The trees and hedging provide architecture in this garden: box-pleached hornbeam at the higher level, and yew hedging to screen the lower part of the tennis court area.

A sketch shows how planting is used to effect to create defined spaces for lounging in this garden adjacent to a spa.

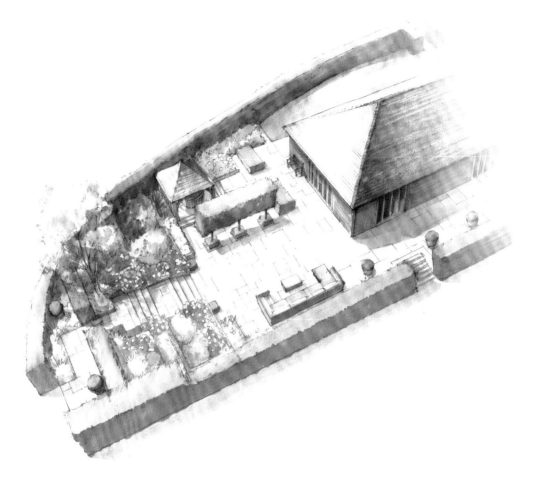

Back to that openness. This spot was situated directly by an enormous tractor shed in constant use, and so the garden needed a real injection of privacy. It's an element that's nearly always in the top three desires on a garden-owner's wish list, but here privacy simply had to be the top, number one. If I were to ask you what comes to mind when you think of ways to create privacy in a garden, you'd probably suggest hedging, trees, walls, and you'd be absolutely spot on. Drilling down on the idea of privacy, and why we want it, we get to the fact that feeling held, embraced, enclosed, protected in a garden space is one of the loveliest feelings of all. We feel safe. We feel confident in our daydreams, and in those daydreams we sense the magic of the garden itself.

And so it was that tall yew hedges went around the perimeter of this space as the pool building was being constructed, then brick walls to create little semi-enclosures, creating nooks and conversation spots as well as, more practically, dealing with various changes of level on the property. These new layers and "rooms" also provided the place for green, more green. For a simple ribbon around the edge of something simply isn't enough. I want interest in terms of elements moving in from either side. The wings, the stage flats that make us pause and hide and screen and pinpoint an atmosphere, from all sorts of angles. To do that, I need green.

In his transcendent book *Chroma*, Derek Jarman remembered words of the fifteenth-century Italian humanist philosopher Marsilio Ficino: "The conversation of old people should be under Venus in a green meadow. While we are strolling through all this greenery, we might ask why the colour green is a sight that helps us more than any other." They knew about forest bathing, even then.

Too often the only synonyms we hear for green are lime, emerald, olive, and chartreuse. Here are

Left: Simple lines and geometric plantings are softened with blousy plants in this sunken garden.

Opposite: Green is ever the colour of restoration and tranquillity. The white birch bark here is highlighted immediately by *Allium* 'Mt. Everest' and subsequently by *Hydrangea arborescens* 'Annabelle'.

some more for starters: apple green, mint green, forest green, bottle green, sage green, jade, moss green, pea green, pine green, seafoam, pistachio, emerald green, khaki, eau de Nil, racing green, verdigris, absinthe, Kelly green, Scheele's green, terra verde, avocado, celadon, celandine, asparagus, beryl, Lincoln green, gaudy, Hooker's green, jasper, malachite, peridot, Phthalo green, peacock green, viridian, mountain green, leek green, grass green, duck green, oil green, siskin. My hope in this project was not only to include a great variety of greens, but to have the patrons sense them, revel subconsciously in their depth, even if they didn't pause to name every single shade.

The refreshing countryside comes to mind when our imaginations go green. It's a colour of restoration and tranquillity. The Latin for green is *viridis*, from the same root as the words for strength and life. A coincidence? That leads us to wonder how green ever came to be associated with envy, spite, or illness.

When did green begin to have negative associations? In a way that is hard for us to understand now, the process of mixing colours in medieval times was viewed with suspicion and actually considered a kind of alchemy, so blue and yellow simply weren't allowed to be mixed. And even when in the early Renaissance it became more acceptable to experiment with colour, artists had to create their own green paints—a difficult undertaking as the pigments used to achieve green were fussy and neither stable nor predictable. Verdigris would blacken; even relatively recent painters such as Georges Seurat had problems with it, and the grass in his *A Sunday Afternoon on the Island of La Grande Jatte* has appeared to "wither" in patches as his chrome yellow darkened. Maybe this is why we link green with poison and evil? The link with poison is certainly justified, as the copper arsenite pigments developed in the nineteenth century were gaily used in clothes and food wrapping... alarmingly poisoning people along the way.

The Green Man

If you've ever had the luck to attend a May festival, or a Morris dance even, you may have noticed a peculiar fellow all dressed in green. It may be the Green Man, Jack in the Green, the symbol of man's reliance on Nature, a symbol of life and of the renewed cycle of growth each spring.

Although the term wasn't coined until the 1930s, the idea of the Green Man has been with us for a long time. Usually depicted as a human but sometimes as an animal, his leaf-and-vine-covered head appears in various forms in India and Asia as well as the British Isles. There's an Irish character called a Derg Corra, meaning "man in the tree," in India Kirtimukha, "the Face of Glory," wards off evil, in Borneo he appears to be a guardian of the forest. Osiris of ancient Egypt, Odin of Norse mythology, the Arthurian Green Knight, harvest season's John Barleycorn, the Holly King, and Thamuz of the Mesopotamians—all are versions of the Green Man.

Green has thankfully taken on once more its time-trusted association with new life. This garden capitalizes on that, providing green, green, and more green at every turn—with a bit of fresh white from *Hydrangea arborescens* 'Annabelle'. Box-pleached hornbeam, a no-brainer of a choice due to the majestic specimens of natural hornbeam in the view beyond, do the job of screening the undesirable elements mentioned previously, as well as creating a blur, a distraction from the tennis court beyond.

You're never going to screen a tennis court. Not easily, at any rate. They're big, they take up volume, and no one really wants to play tennis in a dark, enclosed spot anyway. Best to distract, a concept I picked up on years ago from the British designer James Alexander-Sinclair, who came up with the idea of placing beautiful zigzagging parterre plantings around them—a bit unusual and therefore captivating in a number of ways that keep the eye from going directly to a chain-link fence. The geometric layers here, cubes on stilts and cubes on the ground, are a development of that idea. To add charm, beds full of more hydrangea, evergreen viburnum, pittosporum, and a few multistem silver-barked birches create privacy and diversion in every direction.

Green and white, cool against dark, a classic pairing used in a contemporary way, for clean simplicity as well as privacy. A bit of a nod to the famous White Garden just down the road, this white garden intends to entertain and please, with these layers of green throwing up imaginary walls and screens around the space.

Opposite: Mass plantings of white hydrangeas and architectural foliage including equisetum draws the gaze away from the tennis court beyond the hedge.

Secret Garden in Kent

Taste in art is one of the most subjective of all tastes. A client and I may never come to an agreement on the most beautiful shade of pink, for example, and they are not necessarily going to immediately be drawn to the art I love. When it came to choosing pieces for this garden, however, subjective and objective were obliged to meet. A collector asked to me to place three figurative sculptures by artist Helen Sinclair in a garden space where normally I might think of including one at the most. We did a plausible job of listening to each other, having healthy debates for days, and then we realised it was simply a question of acquiescing to who was really in charge: not me, not the client, but the figures themselves. You see a sculpture, a statue, a piece of art that been given real life by its creator… you simply can't just buy it at an exhibition, drop it in any old green space, and say, "Stay there." I urge you to take a leap, too, and listen to the inanimate.

Figurative pieces have always seemed to me the most difficult to choose—you're going to be sharing your garden with this person for a while, so you need to be sure that you're holding up your side of the friendship by treating them well. Depictions of reality become reality. Don't believe me? Admit silently now whether you've ever found yourself talking to a sculpture in your own garden. When pieces with spirit are invited in, the space becomes theirs as much as ours.

When I first saw this garden, it was essentially a carpark straight off the road in the middle of this beautiful village. My job was to transform it into a place of quiet seclusion, a place to keep these three figures safe and housed as much as on gallerylike display. They deserved a textured, foliage-rich courtyard that would be full of colour and visitors to keep them company. Grandparents, children on tricycles, adults seeking quietude—it had to work for them all.

To create privacy, these sculptures first needed a little shelter. Material choice is easy in a location like this; the historic buildings nearby all give little hints as to their history and purpose, and the vernacular can be celebrated rather than apologised for—the bakery here, the old telegraph exchange over there, relics of a busy, thriving village with the bustle of years gone by still echoing, and so it was that bricks, stones, and timber were suggested into this space, to help this new addition snuggle in immediately. I repurposed old bricks into a new wall for privacy and set a new gate made out of old oak into it. New pavers in the colour of old brick make for a practical dining spot, laid in basketweave to provide just a bit of history and differentiation from brickwork nearby.

As the garden took shape, the three figures all found their spaces. The one with the most upright form stands kindly, as if in welcome, adjacent to the new gate. An element of both surprise and guardianship, it greets all whilst being gently sheltered by a multi-stemmed *Cercis canadensis* 'Forest Pansy', whose satisfying reds and purples translate the brick's palette into a soft leaf form. You don't see the sculpture immediately upon entering—in this garden it's the quiet introvert who doesn't need to speak loudly, but who simply observes and waits patiently

The reds and purples of a multi-stemmed *Cercis canadensis* 'Forest Pansy' translate the brick's palette into a soft leaf form.

to be noticed. Another sculpture sits in meditation at the opposite end of the garden, by ancient oaks and beeches towering above. Just there in the darkness, you catch a glimpse of her, sitting cross-legged on the ground, lost in thought in the shadows.

The idea of allowing a garden's features to reveal themselves slowly, with a measured cadence, is critical to enjoying it even in—or perhaps especially in—a small space. Our eyes see something and send a message to the brain, which then spends a bit of time concentrating on it. As more layers and textures and colours and dappled light are gradually revealed along the way, so we are more and more drawn along to explore further, amused at our own surprise and fascinated by our inability to grasp all at a single glance. We're engaged.

The journey round this garden is led by various focal points and cues as to where to go. We only meet the third sculpture, tucked demurely behind some grasses, when, fittingly, the third of three amelanchiers suggests that we take a turn leading to a quiet spot in front of the sitting room. The last figure sits here, legs dangling from a plinth, in a flurry of the giant oat grass *Stipa gigantea*, its splaying stems echo the forms of the amelanchier, whose blossoms, fruits, and autumn colour move us through the seasons, and even when seemingly bare of anything, have stems that create sculpture in the colours and shapes of the stems, grey and branching against brick-browns.

The foliage of liquidambar and *Cercis canadensis* 'Forest Pansy' enhance the pleasantly rusty tones of the terrace's basketweave brick pavers.

Above: Foliage layers frame views of sculptures by Helen Sinclair, including a seated figure half-hidden amongst the plants. Plants were chosen for leaves and branches that catch the light and cast intriguing shadows particularly well.

Opposite: The rustic gate entrance suggests a secret garden.

A Coastal Sussex Garden

With an energetic walk or a quick drive, you could cover a fair stretch of the East Sussex coastline in a day. What's fascinating is how much that coastline changes from mile to mile. The sea powers everything. It's omnipresent. I certainly can't hope to move it or screen it or ignore it in the service of creating a garden. Its strength, its movement, the force that it brings with it as the winds and salt smash onto the shore and change its form every day: paying homage to those elements is where any design here must start. The tides move everything around on the ground and in our minds, with altering skyscapes and shingle-scapes as low spring tides reveal treasures and subsequent neap tides pull the ocean out farther than we swear we've ever seen it go, like magic.

This is a garden for clients full to the brim with creativity, who themselves spend their working days conjuring up imaginary scenes, and who were defeated by an inherited mess of plastic grass and rendered rectilinear walls. The idea of borrowing from the landscape became quite literal to fix all that. We decided to look for items that had washed up near to the house or were adrift, figuring we're just gently borrowing them for a while, placing them upon a shelf inside the boundary palisade, before they're eventually set back where they were found. There was no digging or excavating or disturbance of habitat—but we gladly accepted anything that appeared, high and dry, on loan from the sea library.

In this wild, wind-battered spot by the sea, anything too clearly machine-geometric or in a material that had been engineered by humans to

A place to relax, open and yet hidden at the same time, this garden is tucked away in its coastal setting.

resist weathering would have looked out of place. The untamed nature of the spot dictates tumbles of boulders for structure that seem to have been rolled in by the heaviest of storms at sea; pathways are a jigsaw of Purbeck stone in crazy paving detail, rugged. The "gribbled" reclaimed timber fence planks are from a disused pier, their rearranged form inspired by groynes nearby. Repurposed here, they have now found a home by the sea once more, in a coastal garden in a different place, but not too far from where they were originally erected.

Details, more than grand gestures, make a space feel authentic.

Creating shelter in a reclaimed space had resulted in a green space for a family. Resilient grasses and rosemary have shades muted enough to settle in amongst other tough plants that don't seem to mind the constant onslaught of wind, salt, and sun. They spill out of nooks and crannies, gently buffering places to think, places to lounge, and places to play. This garden is in no way looking to hide from exposure, just to shelter us from it for a little while.

Opposite: Bespoke Purbeck stone crazy paving (left) is edged with boulders from the same quarry, whilst reclaimed timber is used as a weathered fence (right) that suits and can handle the salty setting.

Above: Tough plants including lavender, erigeron, and red-toned grasses will not only survive but thrive along the coast.

Restoring a Victorian Walled Garden

Many of us say autumn is our favourite season. The morning light throws a hazy veil over everything as mists hang low in the garden in the early hours. Spiders spin their webs, not always helpfully across paths and you can get caught up unawares in a cobwebby surprise. But the light, the beauty, the quiet and the softness almost lulls you into accepting that from now on the days will be shorter, and it's hard to imagine the approaching darkness. The harvest has been gathered, wreaths of autumn leaves placed on doors, and the hard labour is done. It's time to start retreating indoors, to reflect on what we've achieved.

With my love of research and history, imagine my delight when I was asked by its custodians, Ian James and Nick Selby, to restore Water Lane's three-acre Victorian walled garden with its array of glasshouses. As it's open to the public already, there's a real opportunity to share the process and progress, to celebrate rebirth in real time as we accomplish the renovation in phases.

The visitor today can wander idly amongst the beds, take moody photos of those glasshouses that haven't yet been renovated and which have almost been reclaimed by Mother Nature, stop casually for something to eat, generally potter and explore for a day out. A century ago, this garden would have been busy with the activity of forty gardeners who worked the vegetable patches, tended the carnation house and the pelargonium house, kept the melon house at just the right temperature to produce exotic fruit.

A late-summer border gently brings this Victorian walled garden into the twenty-first century.

Walking around at dawn, the sun low in the sky as high summer moves away from us and thoughts turn to harvest, the spirit of the place makes itself felt. You catch a glimpse of someone with a garden trug out the corner of your eye, swear you can hear a wooden wheelbarrow trundling by. You wonder whether you're in the present or the past, so real the spirits of the place appear to be, reminding us of the legacy of those who went before.

There is an inherent romance to this garden imbued by a long trail of stories and history and, until lately, benign neglect. There's much to do as I work together with Nick and Ian on plans to gently tease out what the garden wants to give us—we all agree the romance should stay. It's an exciting and definitely ambitious, long-term opportunity to restore this back to being a fully productive garden. But it is not

to be a pastiche of Victoriana. We are respecting its roots; the aim from now on is that the garden will be made accessible to all, attractive to a wide audience with new layers of purpose and contemporary functions. The restoration will take many years, we know this, and it will happen in phases, to fulfil an intent to create a democratic place where people can come and learn and where skilled teachers can share their knowledge in horticulture, floral design, and many kinds of artisan crafts and cookery.

Any urgency is tempered by a strong sense of responsibility—we have to respect past glory as well as make it a sustainable, inspirational, and welcoming garden for the twenty-first century and beyond. Planned interventions include a rose "orchard" with a bulb meadow below, a quince tree avenue leading through the green gates at the pedestrian entrance,

perennial and stock beds in the south quadrant, follies and wall borders, a wisteria cascade, a children's nature play area, a forest garden and sculpture trail, a nuttery, and educational spaces. Paths form a labyrinth within themselves to enable visitors to choose to how to explore this garden and encourage them to explore and linger.

Thinking about visitors leads to thoughts of the times of year when most people might pass through; in the United Kingdom, September is nearly always a much better, more predictable weather month than May, so it's a question of whether to lean into a lovely autumn palette as a showstopper, holding the nerve and avoiding a mad dash for early-season colour that could be taken down by a squall in a single afternoon. Seasonal light also changes colour—will muted highlights and colourwashes, seed heads and waving

This Victorian walled garden contains many treasures, including one of the longest peach cases in the United Kingdom; deciding how much to restore versus what to retain as it is now is an ongoing conversation.

Overleaf: The gentlest of interventions: bales of hay form a simple but beguiling seating area in a mown patch of grass.

grasses feel sympathetic in some sense with the faded relics all around? If so, we should look to the last of the repeat-flowering roses, nerines, species dahlias—selected carefully to avoid a soupy jumble of colour and texture—ruby-magenta tassels of amaranth, and then mounds of foliage shining out autumn colour. A sense of genteel mellowness, no one bloom in a hurry to go anywhere.

Water Lane is part of the original Tongswood Estate. The name "Tongswood" originates from the two forks (*tangs* in Old English) of the River Rother that ran through the property, and as the contemporary name infers, water still plays significant role in this site. Imagine how much rain could be captured as it sheets off that mass of pitched roofs. To capture it was the first impulse, which led to water circulation as an important theme for the new design; it could manifest along a visible path, with both water source and water storage on show,

and we could highlight its interim destination in the original circular dipping pond, which still stood at the centre of the garden's four quadrants. The water would be directed from there to a mass of stock beds, display beds, beds for cut flowers headed for table-tops and bridal bouquets, beds for salad leaves that will then make their way via the kitchen to plates.

We're operating on no-dig principles, and compost stands as a core part of making the soil good again. No chemicals are used. Layers of productive shrubs and trees are a favourite way of making the grouping of plants both beautiful as well as useful. Edible hedges here will work in rows and just-discernible layers in this luxury of space. Regeneration and sustainability are part of every facet of this design, the underpinnings of an approach with respect at its heart; with this respect, all the romance of a bygone era allows itself to bloom again.

Late-blooming flowers help to fulfil the garden's mission of drawing visitors late into the season. Opposite, top: *Dahlia* 'Verrone's Obsidian'. Opposite, bottom: *Dahlia* 'La Recoleta'. Above: *Dahlia* 'Bacardi'.

Above: A sea of cosmos and *Dahlia merckii* add romance to the late-summer season. Opposite: As blooms and long grasses fade to autumnal tones, they flatter the beauty, scale, and colour of the old brick walls.

Repairing the Land

Whatever size the patch of earth that comes with our home, we would do well to remember that we've been *entrusted* with it. It's precious, on loan from Mother Nature, and given to us to look after well. It's guardianship, rather than ownership, no matter what our temporary paper records say. We have a duty to keep it up—and I don't mean duty in the sense of a burden, all weeding and chores. There's so much fun to be had in nurturing, and there is so much to nurture within one garden space; the garden takes it many steps further as there are so many living things within one place, if you think that within the soil itself there are thousands upon thousands of the tiniest living things. It's a community, a nation, a world of stuff to care for. We've got to know how to treat it.

When a house has a name, and the house's name was once the still-thriving busy village's name, there's a whole lot of unspoken history laying there, waiting to be rediscovered. In this village, a war memorial stands at the crossroads. A church to one side. Rudyard Kipling lived around the corner from here; his house Bateman's is still open to visitors, and is where he wrote "The Glory of the Garden," a poem celebrating the idea that the garden, and the country as a whole, is a beautiful thing indeed, if looked after and supported by its people.

Smugglers, as it happens, thrived here in Burwash, East Sussex; the "owlers" as they were called, had done a robust business for generations. There's a smuggler's grave in the churchyard across the way. Highwaymen alternately idled and sprung into action on the village road. Eight miles away lies Senlac Hill, where in 1066 Harold Godwinson deployed his army against William and his conquerors. The ghosts of men are around.

This garden was designed to be truly romantic—as well as to be kept up by a client who had never gardened before.

Above and opposite: To keep maintenance to a minimum, the garden includes a range of disease-resistant English roses, including *Rosa* Olivia Rose Austin (= 'Ausmixture'), *R.* Gentle Hermione (= 'Ausrumba'),

R. Munstead Wood (= 'Ausbernard'), *R.* Falstaff (= 'Ausverse'), and *R.* 'Queen Elizabeth'. All have the UK native *Valeriana officinalis* as a lofty planting partner in early summer.

Overleaf: A pair of deep flowerbeds conceal a tree seat. Along with a couple of benches, this is all that's been introduced in this garden full of tumbling, rambling plants.

In this garden, I look for clues to match the intents of those who came before with those who asked me to help them create this garden, and I knew the new inhabitants well. When Mary Jane Paterson and I first met, she was a terrible gardener and I was a terrible cook. Years later, her gardening skills are pretty brilliant, as seen in the transformation of her own garden, which we undertook whilst accidentally writing a book at the same time. Working with what was there, making do and mending where I could, a regenerative approach, as ever, led to the transformation of a romantic atmosphere enveloping this beautiful historic house.

The planting is simple, easy to understand and approachable for someone who hasn't gardened before. No hard edges, all simple and soft. It's on the wilder side of natural—its owner describes it as "hairy." One or two roses continue to pop up unexpectedly like those highwaymen, appearing only when it befits their self-interested whims: *Rosa* Olivia Rose Austin (= 'Ausmixture') drops a flower here, *R.* Gertrude Jekyll (= 'Ausboard') manages to send out a last missive over there. Valerian, with its long history of use in love potions and against curses and nefarious goings-on, rejoices consistently here as if in moral defiance. We anthropomorphise plants, assigning them personality, because we understand that they inevitably behave in a way botany alone cannot explain.

An edict of "no overthinking" led to a ramble and tangle of perennials, just the way I like them. No chemicals. There's no need. A smattering of pink is an uplifting, happy-making thing indeed. Here in the tumbling flowerbeds, the few soft pink roses sit happily amongst the spires of purple salvia and lavender veronicastrum, verticals that take up watch over the place as the wheel of the year moves round and catches the lowering light. Just walking into this garden, you can sense it's tended lovingly rather than obsessively, and it makes you feel good. And as for the bees and all the other pollinators, they're beside themselves with buzzing busy-ness as they zoom from plant to plant in this feast of a border.

A pair of flowerbeds, a tree seat, and a bench or two—this is all that's been introduced in this garden. Any more, and the place wouldn't have felt balanced; instead it would have been clear that it had been me, the upstart visitor, telling the garden what I expected, not what it required or wanted. There's a fine balance, but as the idealistic impositions are weeded out, the garden thanks us and lets us know that it's okay. A path leads us round to greet the trees; the trees greet the dawn and say goodbye at sunset.

A Garden within a Garden

Rosemoor is a Royal Horticultural Society garden that sits in a valley in the heart of Devon. The sun can shine brightly on the South West Peninsula, but this stretch of land also receives high rainfall. And so when I first visited, it was muddy, and the sky held only shades of grey and dirty neutrals. Every inch was wet.

Mud, and rain, and cold. The rain powered down as we walked along the steely backbone of yew that sets out the individual compartments that go to make up this space. The cold was driving down into bones, and you just knew that was going to take more than a lunch by a fire to get the heat back again to where it should be.

Green hedges loomed black in the smothered light, enclosing a spot that felt moody and brooding. The unforgiving, impenetrable black tarmac, thirty years old, provided the perfect surface for rainwater to skid down along and then puddle up on top of as its search for an outlet proved fruitless. The irony in all of this is that just beyond the garden there's a tapestry of greens in a woodland that scrambles down the slopes of the River Torridge, the obvious destination for the rain, which instead was being trapped and pooled in dirty, sludgy patches of wet.

And so it was, soaked in the drizzle of that uncompromising day, that the atmosphere this garden needed to have started to reveal itself. Getting into the mind of a client when there is no identifiable client creates an interesting conundrum; in a private garden I meet the person who is the current guardian of that space, I get to know them, and we have plenty of cups of tea whilst we hammer out

Winter frost only enhances
the structure of the plants
in the Cool Garden at RHS
Rosemoor in Devon.

Imbolc

January is a cold old month. After the relentless push of Christmas and then the inevitable
slump as our less-distracted minds look outside, it's easy to get a bit down in the dumps
about this greyest time of year. Battleship-
grey skies taunt us; we *know* what hovers just
above those really annoying clouds. So we
grumble and wait for the days to get longer.

And bit by bit, they do. The Wheel of the Year
starts to make itself felt—*Imbolc* is the Gaelic
word for this slow moment between the
winter and spring equinoxes. As the relentless
cold makes us wonder for a moment whether
it will ever end, we begin to find signs here
and there that all is not quite as hopeless as
it may sometimes seem, and that everything
goes on. Frost is cold, but it will get warm
again. It's dark, but every day we're given just
a precious minute more of light. The dawn
chorus grows just a little louder, and, as if by
magic—for it really seems like sorcery—out
come the bravest shoots and tips of buds,
sensing with wisdom beyond ours that it's
time.

Frost backlit by winter sun
casts into sharp contrast
the various forms of plants
visitors might remark for
their colour only in other
seasons: tightly bunched
foliage, loose stalks, straight
stems, and open branches.

what can and what must and what really shouldn't
happen. In a public space such as this, though,
things are very different. It's a green place for all and
has myriad requirements forced upon it: a place to
potter with a friend, a place to be a little bit quiet, a
place where you might strike up a conversation with
someone new. A place where you introduce a young
child to the embrace of nature. A place where you
sit, a place where you walk, a place you experience in
a powered wheelchair.

The place also has to make sense for the gardeners who will maintain it. It has to make sense for
those who are out in every weather making sure that
the plants thrive, and before that, working alongside the designer to make those concepts a reality
by, in their own way, getting into the head of the
designer by perhaps interpreting the plant names
and atmosphere adjectives that get bandied about,
and suggesting other plants that might also do the
job. When it makes sense to its guardians, they
begin to have a sense of what the garden is going to
wind up being about before it is even a scribble on a
piece of paper, before the designer knows it herself
sometimes.

All of these factors coming from all directions—
the practicalities, the requirements, the demands,
the needs, the purpose, the result—must be taken
into consideration in order for a garden to work.
And nowhere more so than here, a place open to the
public in every weather.

When you visit a garden, there's always one element that stands out even just a little bit more than
anything else, and once you've recognised it, everything
else starts to fall into place. It requires a bit of listening to your heart or your gut, whichever drives you;
don't ignore a niggling feeling, as it might be the very
thing that sparks the garden, that the garden centres
its whole self around. Here, it was the rain. I suddenly
wanted to harness it, save it, use it, reuse it. Beauty
and consideration had to proceed hand in hand, not
compete, each as valid a presence as the other.

With this revelation I found hope; I could see green shoots and bright spring light. I could convince myself to make the most of what the space already had and to rely on the ways that others once used to manage their outside places as guidance. Regeneration, we call it. It's an approach that sometimes oddly used to be termed "sustainability," but this has since lost its meaning by being greenwashed into a vague, fluffy sense of doing good. To sustain means to nurture, to keep on; I see this as "make do and mend," but there's an endgame which seemed to get lost in all that easy-speak, there was a lack of a word to describe what it was all about. Regeneration bundles up the ideas of being kind, nurturing, continuing, taking care of something, being thoughtful, considerate, loving—everything that a gardener is and does. Looking after the soil, avoiding chemicals is with the aim of regenerating the land, using what we have and providing habitats and food in the process.

These are notions when we're looking at a garden space, whether it's a patch of land, an opening in the paving by your doorstep, or a bigger space that takes in trees and whole acres, that are to keep in mind while surveying what we have. Taking stock and understanding what there is, and that *whatever* is there can almost always be considered an asset, can be the very first step in a kind, considerate approach to shaping space, giving it a feeling, a meaning, a character that feels authentic. A true atmosphere.

Here, my mind darted back to beauty experienced elsewhere, the idea that channelling water is in itself an interesting feat of engineering. I recalled cobbled drainage gulleys that wind along and down the streets of Montmartre in Paris, children splashing in them—purpose *and* play. The structural design feature revealed itself in a nutshell to me. This garden would need to embrace all that rainfall rather than battle against it. It would celebrate it, in fact, making the most of an element that's vital but currently an inconvenience.

Essentially, drawing lines along the existing slopes created this garden. Rainfall into river into lake—there's the concept. Spouts direct water from a wall made of local stone into an upper tank; from here wind rills of granite setts glistening into a film of water which skirts their surface, deliberately uneven to slow down the pace of anyone who decides to go for a bit of an enthusiastic paddle. Taking their cue from how water behaves and absorbs in wilder places, these rills and channels appear and vanish, directing the journey and creating handy bridges in the process. Eventually, the waters all come together in a pond at the bottom of this site. The curving geometry imposed on a piece of land that had started out flat could feel odd, but here it clearly emulates the wonderful wooded slopes just beyond. The hedging-as-enclosure compels visitors to wander through and around and along the rills: to me, that's what a garden is for.

It functions as an all-year-round garden despite climatic vagaries in the sense that it changes over the months. On a spring day the bulbs scatter at ground level, inviting you to get up close; on a hot summer's day it really is a cool place to be as you try to resist dipping at least a toe in the rills and channels. In winter, all the moisture around means frost, and this highlights the purposefully highly structural shapes of the evergreen plants and personality-rich grasses and seedheads in a magical way while turning the palette cool and emulating the high-and-low height hierarchy of the forest canopy beyond.

And to end on the most important part: I designed this garden to be truly accessible. I sometimes still potter in as a mystery shopper; I watch mobility scooters making their way easily around, three-point turns and all. I watch as children dip their feet into the canals and rills, ignoring their parents' instructions not to, in blazing temperatures when paddling and Poohsticks are the order of the day. I'm happy.

244

This composition of forms—
spheres, low waving grasses,
upright branching habits—
shows how taking geometry
into consideration when
planting can extend a garden's
season of interest.

ACKNOWLEDGMENTS

Thank you to every single client who has ever entrusted me with your garden. For coming along on the ride, for allowing me to explore the possibilities and for believing in the dreams. I love every single one of these gardens, and they've become reality because of your trust and your hopes—and all those cups of tea. We did it together.

None of these spaces would exist without all the growers and landscapers who work tirelessly in all weathers to make these dreams come true, and to all those skilled gardeners who look after these gardens.

A big thank you to David Austin Roses for all the inspiration.

Stacee Lawrence, you have the patience of a saint and you deserve a medal—thank you for navigating me through the editing of this book.

Naomi and Rosanna, you are the very best team I could hope to work with. Every day is a privilege. Kelly, Luisa, and Helen, your patience knows no ends.

This book goes beyond how to design a garden, and there were times when I wondered how I was going to catch all those invisible threads: Andrew Fisher Tomlin, thank you for speaking sense and being the best of sounding boards.

Opportunity allows a designer to create and a writer to write. I've had so many opportunities throughout my life and I appreciate every single one. From the very beginning, thank you to those primary school teachers who encouraged the dreaming and the flights of fancy; thank you for pretending to believe me even when you knew my tallest of tales couldn't possibly be true. It's because of you that I love writing. To Sir John Hale, Simon Pyle, and Rosemary Alexander: the gardens I create look the way they do because of what I've learned from you.

To my children, George and Cecilia, as ever, thank you for putting up with me while I worked on this book—in fact, thank you for putting up with me while I've been working on these gardens, which I know has literally been your Forever. You're the best.

And to my mother and father, thank you for introducing me to the magic of places, for your constant encouragement, and for giving me every opportunity. Opportunity really is a gift to be treasured, and I know just how lucky I am.

PHOTOGRAPHY CREDITS

Maria Bell: 224, 232

Camera Press Ltd / Alamy: 28 top

Marianne Cartwright-Hignett: 190 all

Ben Davies: 150, 153 bottom, 154 top, 154 bottom, 156–57

Katy Donaldson: 17 top, 17 bottom left, 17 bottom right, 20 left, 20 right, 76, 78, 79, 82 left, 99 all, 180, 182 top, 182 bottom, 183 all, 184, 185 left, 185 right

GAP Photos: 82 right

GAP Photos/Annie Green-Armytage: 81 top, 83

GAP Photos/Marcus Harpur: 81 bottom, 166, 168, 169, 170, 171 top, 171 bottom

GAP Photos/Andrea Jones: 153 top

GAP Photos/Joanna Kossak: 80

GAP Photos/Anna Omiotek-Tott: 155

Marcus Harpur: 214, 216, 218 all, 219

Jason Ingram: 5, 52, 54, 55, 56, 57, 58 top, 58 bottom left, 58 bottom right, 85, 86, 87, 88, 89 all, 90–91, 93, 108, 110, 111 top, 111 bottom, 112, 113 all, 115, 116, 117, 118 all, 119 left, 119 right, 120–21, 192, 194 left, 194 right, 195, 196 all, 197, 198, 199, 226, 227 left, 227 right, 228–29, 230 top, 230 bottom, 231, 233, 234, 236 all, 237, 238–39, 240, 243, 245

Courtesy Jo Thompson Landscape & Garden Design: 48, 69, 152, 177 bottom, 209

© MMGI / Marianne Majerus: 60, 62, 63, 64, 65 all

Clive Nichols: 186, 189 top right, 189 bottom

Will Scott Photography Ltd: 102, 104, 105, 106 top, 106 bottom, 107

Rachel Warne: 2, 6, 7 left, 7 right, 9, 10, 12–13, 15 left, 15 right, 18, 24–25, 26, 28 bottom, 29, 30–31, 32, 33 left, 33 right, 34, 35, 36, 38–39, 40 left, 40 right, 41, 42 top, 42 bottom, 45, 46, 49, 50, 51, 66, 68, 71, 72, 73 top, 74 bottom, 74 left, 74 right, 75, 94, 96–97, 98 left, 98 right, 100–101, 122, 125, 126, 127, 128 top, 128 bottom, 129, 130, 133, 134, 135 all, 136, 138 all, 140, 141, 142, 144–45, 146, 147, 149, 158, 160, 161 all, 163, 164–65, 172, 175, 176, 177 top, 178 left, 178 right, 179, 188 all, 189 top left, 200, 202 left, 202 right, 203, 204–5, 206, 208 top, 208 bottom, 210, 211, 213 all, 220, 222 left, 222 right, 223 left, 223 right

First published in the United States of America in 2025 by
Rizzoli International Publications, Inc.
49 West 27th Street
New York, NY 10001
www.rizzoliusa.com

Publisher: Charles Miers
Editor: Stacee Gravelle Lawrence
Design: Susan Evans, Design per se
Production Manager: Alyn Evans
Managing Editor: Lynn Scrabis

ISBN: 978-0-8478-4675-7
Library of Congress Control Number: 2024947062

Printed in China
2025 2026 2027 2028 / 10 9 8 7 6 5 4 3 2 1

Visit us online:
Instagram.com/RizzoliBooks
Facebook.com/RizzoliNewYork
X: @Rizzoli_Books
Youtube.com/user/RizzoliNY